Joe The Plumber

Fighting for the American Dream

Joe The Plumber

Fighting for the American Dream

by Samuel J. Wurzelbacher
with Thomas N. Tabback

PearlGate Publishing

JOE THE PLUMBER
Fighting for the American Dream

A PearlGate Publishing Book – Austin, TX
Copyright © 2008 PearlGate Publishing, LLC
All rights reserved.

Library of Congress Control Number (LCCN): 2008911441

ISBN-10: 0-9769740-3-7
ISBN-13: 978-0-9769740-3-1

Published in the United States of America
Printed and Published simultaneously in Canada

PearlGate and colophon are trademarks of PearlGate Publishing, LLC

Jacket design, artwork, logos and photographs copyright © 2008 by PearlGate Publishing, LLC
www.pearlgatepublishing.com

11 10 9 8 7 6 5 4 3 2   SECOND EDITION

CONTENTS

FOREWORD

My Friend Joe

I first met Samuel J. Wurzelbacher over a phone call on October 18, 2008, just three days after that fateful and final presidential debate where Senators McCain and Obama teamed up to make *Joe The Plumber* a national working-class icon. Like most of America, I was intrigued by his story, but also instinctively felt there was something more behind this unassuming man from Ohio than we had yet seen in the media. I am very pleased to have found that I was right.

Joe was in Central Park in New York, enjoying his first trip to the Big Apple before his scheduled appearance on *Huckabee*. We talked for an hour or so to determine whether he had a story that he wanted to tell America, and what sort of story I was capable of helping him tell. He wasted no time in confronting me about my financial motivations. I told him that if we told a good story, a story worth telling, then money was not something about which to be concerned. I later found out that, despite being approached by other writer and publisher suitors, he chose me, because my focus was not about "cashing in" as he put it. Ironically, during our discussion, I was interviewing him just as much as he was interviewing me. I learned that we had similar core beliefs, not so much about politics, but about the American Dream and the guiding hand of fate, which we both recognize is God.

When I finally met Joe a few days later in his hometown of Holland, Ohio, we were like longtime pen pals meeting face-to-face for the first time. He was warm and humble, but firm in his beliefs and committed to his morals and values. Although I was a stranger, Joe and his family welcomed me into their home and cared for me as one of their own. For that, they will always hold a special place in my heart.

The subsequent days and weeks I accompanied Joe along the media circuit and campaign trail is something I'll never forget. I could write 500 pages on the subject and not do it justice. It was as mentally challenging for him, as it was spiritually. However, I never once saw Joe compromise his principles in return for ill-gotten gains. This display of moral certitude and inner strength quickly earned my respect.

Above all, I was most impressed with Joe's equally magnetic and magnanimous nature. The finest example of this quality occurred during a long walk we took one day, just prior to his public endorsement of McCain. We came upon a home with a giant-sized *Obama for President 2008* sign spanning nearly the entire length of its roof. In the front yard a mature and stylish black woman raked leaves along with the help of her son, a man about Joe's age.

When she saw Joe, she put her hands on her hips, cocked her head and said, "Are you *the* Joe The Plumber?"

"Darlin'," Joe replied, "you know darn well I am." Without hesitation he walked over to her and she gave him a warm and affectionate hug. Her son walked over and shook Joe's hand, again with affection and respect.

Come to find out, Joe had grown up across the street from this woman and her children had been his childhood playmates. She told him how awful she felt about what certain elements of the media and political machines were doing to him, which was a common theme amongst many Obama supporters I witnessed him meet. She also told him that she felt God had a special purpose for him and that, no matter what, he needed to follow it. It was a rare and emotional moment, and I was honored to have shared in it.

Within the pages of this book you will not be disappointed by Joe's trademark pull-no-punches opinions on various matters. Whether you agree with him or not, I think you will appreciate his candor, but also his caring nature to his family, his neighbors and · strangers like you and me. For me, Joe is what America is all about. He is real. His life is real. The experiences that have shaped him are real. Regardless of your political affiliations or proclivities, Joe is the kind of guy that would give you the shirt from off his back and the food from off his plate. He is the kind of guy we would all cherish to call our neighbor.

Joe, here's to you *brother* . . .

—*Thomas N. Tabback*
Your Friend

It's a weird feeling to be writing a dedication. Never would I have dreamed in a million years that I would be doing this. Nonetheless, here I am . . .

To God . . .

I have been blessed with the company of many great people in my life. For that, and many more reasons, I would like to thank God. Throughout my life God has always been there for me. When in doubt, I turn to God. When I need guidance, I turn to God. When I need strength, again, I turn to God. Without God in my life, I would have been lost down a dark and lonely road long ago. Thank you God, from your humble servant Joe.

To My Son, Joey . . .

Being your Dad has brought me complete JOY and Happiness. I could not imagine my life without you. I love our playtime together, whether playing sports in the front yard or just horsing around. I love teaching you about God, life, and the things you will need to know in order to become a Great Christian man. I love you son.

To My Mom . . .

Mom, you are incredible!! Thank you for instilling in me your common sense and work ethic. To this day, I don't know anyone who could outwork you. Thank you for your support and Love, for I don't know where I would be in life without you. I love you Mom.

To My Dad . . .

Dad, you are the smartest and Wisest man I know. Thank you for your discipline and guidance. Thank you for marrying my Mom, taking my brother and I in, and making us a family. Thank you for being my Dad. I love you.

PREFACE

I'm Just Joe

I am Samuel J. Wurzelbacher, though you may know me as *Joe The Plumber*. I am a plumber, or at least I was content to be one. Today, I must be the most famous unemployed person in America. Being jobless would normally be a source of shame and enormous discontent, but I have been given a blessing. I have been given a voice, where so many like me have been silenced by the powers of media and political agendas that have culminated in the form of what I believe is an increasingly oppressive government. Don't misunderstand me, because I love my country and the principles for which it stands. Nonetheless, the ideals that gave birth to this nation have been gradually chipped away over the years, and I fear that one day my son or his children, or his children's' children will never know the greatness that was the American Dream.

I decided to do this book, because I wanted to share my true story—the one that was both hidden and disregarded in the midst of the massive shadow of the media spotlight. It's a story that doesn't fit within the nice and tidy packaging of party politics and the power brokers that seek to control the public's thought and opinion. Is it a conspiracy? Probably, but I'm not a *Big Conspiracy* theorist. I call things the way I see them, and I see in black and white, right or wrong. I will be the first one to tell you that it can be difficult to see through the fog of misinformation and confounding agendas, especially when the eyes of America and perhaps the world are upon you. Perception is most often reality to people. They either hear what they want to hear, or they listen to those who tell them what they want to hear. For those of you who have your mind set on an opinion about me, I urge you to keep an open mind until after you have read this book, whether you like me or you don't. I was raised with a set of values that seem to be getting rarer with each new generation. I try to judge as I would like to be judged, which is to measure people by their deeds. I admit I am far from perfect in this regard, but I endeavor to be better. We all must understand that the sum of media sound bites on television, radio or print do not sum up the person, nor do the words of pundits whose opinions are typically well formed and inflexible.

So who is Joe The Plumber? Well, I can tell you that *he* is the creation of the mega-media branding machine. *He* is a banner, a t-shirt, a button and a slogan. *He* is the champion of Middle America. Really, *He* is just a man, who puts his pants on one leg at a time like the rest of you. *He* is nothing extraordinary, but *he* has been thrust into extraordinary events that are staggering in scope and defy the wildest of average imagination. *I* am just like you, and if you can imagine how uncomfortable and unnerving it would be to have every aspect of your life's history examined beneath the microscope, then you have just begun to understand my new reality.

Everything you need to know about me can be summed up in one word—Family. I believe in service; to family, to friends, to neighbors and to country. The Bible teaches us that we are all brothers and sisters, and that is exactly what I believe. In a family, you have a God-given duty to one another. If you see your brother or sister stumble, give them your steady hand. If they fall, lift them up. If they hunger, give them bread, and when they thirst give them drink. This is not just who I am, but many of you as well. Ironically, before this experience I had been much more cynical about the charity and good will of America. I thought that the moral compass of this country had gone askew and that it would take a miracle to bring it back. I was wrong to lose hope. I have many of you to thank for showing me that the heart of our country remains strong, and that we need only band together to see its greatness restored.

It's true, we live in the midst of tough and challenging times of historic proportions, probably unequalled since the Great Depression. But more than our economic struggles, or our fight against terror across the world, or our efforts to keep our growing enemies at bay, I believe we are at a crossroads that will likely determine the fate of our nation. Ask any historian, and he or she will tell you that every superpower from the beginning of time was not destroyed by a threat from afar, but by its own hand from within. We may disagree about which forces may be responsible for threatening our great republic, but I rarely meet someone who does not believe that a storm is nearing. For me, it boils down to *Values* and the American system of government that is guided by them. Without our distinct American Values, we will become the Europe of the mid-twentieth century. You may recall that one man brought all of Europe and nearly the entire world under his noose during that era. His name was Adolf Hitler. Perhaps we should be asking ourselves, who will be the Hitler of our time, or will the next Great War be fought by our children, and are we equipping them with the proper tools necessary for their survival. I guarantee you machines of war alone will not save us. In the end it will come down to *Values*, and who is willing to make the ultimate sacrifice to defend them.

Now you are just beginning to get to know the *Joe* before you met the *Joe* that had the audacity to ask some direct questions of a presidential candidate. Everywhere I go today people say to me, "Joe, you did great! You did the right thing. Keep up the good work." Believe it or not, whether Democrat or Republican, that is what people say. It's surprising to me, and I don't pretend to understand exactly why it is. I do think that a great part of it has to do with the fact that most people are flat out tired of *bait-and-switch-politics*. How many promises must be broken before we wake up and demand something more? How many scandals must go unanswered or crimes unpunished before we can't suffer one more? But what are we really to do? Like many of you, I used to be content with complaining about it, and then relegating myself to usually one of two disappointing options in the voting booth. This experience, however, has taught me that the real power for *real change* is in your own hand and in your own voice. The outpouring of support and encouragement from many of you has caused me to ignore my better judgment and continue to speak out. I may not be as smart as the politicians in Washington, but I know B.S. when I hear it, and if given the chance to look someone in the eye, I know when they have my best interests at heart.

You may ask, "So who do you think you are Joe, a crusader? Do you really think you speak for all of Middle America?" To be quite honest, no. I don't just see myself as ordinary. I am ordinary. I'm as simple as they come, a regular and normally very private guy. I'm a working man. I hardly look past the day before me, what the job will require and how to balance work with the joys and needs of family and friends. As I have said, I'm all about family. I live to provide for my family, and I would sacrifice all that I have for them, especially for my son. In my son I find the true purpose and meaning of life. More than anything in the world, I want to be a father to him and to see him grow into a man in his own right. He is the future of our country and all who live in it, just as your children are. In all our lives there is nothing that comes remotely close to the responsibility we have to them. If ever you question my motives, remember that.

At present, I have yet to find balance with my newfound fame. I still find it hard to believe I'm actually *doing a book*. It's even comical to me at times, though I have come to understand that I have a civic duty to fulfill. Those of you reading this book may think, *Here's Joe, cashing in on his 15 minutes of fame*. Some of you who met me on the street urged me to do exactly that. Nevertheless, those who know me well would tell you that I really don't care for money. Sure, I need some of it like everybody else, but my fortune came when I became a father to my son. No creation of man on this earth could ever come close. No, I am sharing my story because I believe in my son's future, and I want to do my part to help secure and defend the American Dream. Whether you agree or disagree with my views, I hope you respect my earnestness and sincerity.

Joe The Plumber

Fighting for the American Dream

1

Meeting Barack Obama

Sunday, October 12, 2008 started out on the wrong foot at the Wurzelbacher house. It had been a long tough week at work that didn't come to a close until late Saturday night. I was whooped something fierce and couldn't have been dragged out of bed if the house were on fire. Mom, dad and my son Joey were ready enough, but I was dead as a rock. Consequently, my late rise caused the family to miss church, and that really bummed everyone out. To us, church is more than a time to worship. It's an opportunity to share our faith in God with friends and neighbors, the people we love. No excuses though, it was my fault, and perhaps my slothfulness invited the troublesome encounter that would come later that day and would haunt my steps for weeks.

After a short breakfast we all decided to do some fall cleaning and yard work in the back. Wurzelbachers can't sit still, even when there is no work to be done, which wasn't the case. As we tended to the yard, my dad, my son and I reveled in the victory of the Toledo Rockets over the Big-Ten Michigan Wolverines on a fourth-quarter 48-yard field goal—HUGE UPSET! We worked quickly, because we didn't want to miss the opening Kickoff of the Bengals versus Jets game after lunch. Yes, I humbly admit that I have been a loyal Bengals fan through thick and thin since about the age of nine.

Foolish as it may be, I'm just loyal that way about a whole host of lost causes. Dare we hope that our beloved Bengals would achieve their first win of the season against Brett Favre and the Jets? Sure, why not?

With our chores complete, we fixed some turkey sandwiches for lunch and sat down to watch our hopes dashed by Favre as he led the Jets in delivering another sound beating to the Bengals. By halftime, it seemed evident that hope was once again futile. Rather than sulk and complain about their lack-luster performance, my son, Joey and I decided to head out front to toss around the football and enjoy the beautiful warm, sunny day.

It wasn't long before we noticed a hundred or so people migrating down the street, with a constant flow of neighbors emerging from their homes to join the crowd. No one seemed to know what was going on. Maybe a car accident? Kids fighting? Naturally my son and his best friend, two thirteen-year-old boys were fit to be tied, and I released them down the street to investigate.

Shortly, the boys returned and reported that it wasn't an accident or a fight. It wasn't someone leaping tall buildings in a single bound. No, it wasn't someone more powerful than a speeding locomotive either. It was none other than presidential hopeful Barack Obama.

My first reaction was identical to my son and his friend's. I thought, *Wow, a presidential candidate coming out to our little middle-class neighborhood to talk to the people.* I honestly thought it was pretty cool. I had long held the view that my class, the middle-class, was underappreciated and ignored despite our vast contributions to our country, and by extension the world. Therefore, I respected that Senator Obama wanted to come out and talk to average, everyday Americans—my neighbors.

I suppose this story could have ended right there, but something gave me an itch. Initially, my marvel over the situation faded. I'm just like that. I really don't obsess over celebrity of any kind. I continued to play catch with Joey, and really had no further interest. Then, as the senator started canvassing up and down our street with State Troopers and Secret Service in tow, it became apparent that we were not going to be able to continue our game. I admit it was a little frustrating, and that itch began to grow. I studied the scene, taking interest in the security procedure of the Secret Service, as they patted down my many neighbors who crowded before the senator for an opportunity to shake his hand. I measured the faces and sense of excitement throughout the crowd, which was naturally justified. After all, how often does a presidential candidate come into your neighborhood, let alone *the* Barack Obama? Nonetheless, I was struck by the fact that no one was asking any tough questions of this man running for the most powerful office in the world. In fact, it seemed more like a cheerleading session than anything else.

I began to hear myself talking with my friends, boasting about what I would do if ever given the chance to ask a politician a direct question; a real question that a politician couldn't squirm out of answering. My friends would all tell you that I have a deep and concerned interest in politics and government. I was raised to care and understand how important the political system is to our lives. My father taught me from an early age that a people who don't understand their government can easily become enslaved by it. Perhaps that itch came from him, but my friends and family alike would all tell you that what I did next really came as no surprise. "That's just Joe," they would say.

Consequently, I found my feet moving beneath me, and yes, in the direction of the senator. As I neared him, I was quickly and thoroughly patted-down by the Secret Service, which wasn't much to my liking. I was not accustomed to being manhandled. Nonetheless, I was let free to approach the Senator from Illinois and called out loudly above the crowd, "Barack. Hey Barack."

In somewhat of a surreal scene, the senator turned to me and the crowd quieted, parting the way between us as though we had a prearranged meeting. Only a foot and a half from him, I asked in a loud and clear voice, "Do you believe in the American Dream?"

"Yes," he paused, "absolutely." He seemed perplexed and I saw a rare moment of uncertainty in him that I had yet to see anywhere amongst his countless speeches, debates and television interviews.

By now you all know what transpired next, about *spreading the wealth* and *helping the guy behind me*. What most people don't realize is that our discussion went on well beyond that media sound bite. In fact, we had a discussion about *fairness*, since he was suggesting that it is only fair that the wealth in this country give back to those of lesser means. I asked him if he would "be open" to a Flat Tax. His response was yes, but that it would have to be in the vicinity of "forty percent" to satisfy the present size and scope of the Federal Budget. Forty percent! I don't care how much money you make, can you imagine handing over four out of every ten dollars from your paycheck to the Federal Government?

I didn't get a chance to speak my mind, as Barack reacted quickly to my expression and explained that perhaps that figure could be less, maybe twenty-three or twenty-five percent. Still, the damage was done. The back peddling only scared me more. I wondered just what this man would do if given the power to make and enforce public policy. I felt that I had caught a glimpse of what I feared the future might hold under an Obama presidency. Though some of you may watch that footage on the Internet and feel that Barack was forthcoming and genuine, I disagree. If you listen closely and understand just a little about his voting record, you will come to realize that his responses were, in fact, very calculating. This is not just a dig on Obama. I find this to be a common character flaw among most all of our politicians, including McCain—more on that later.

I had been leaning towards McCain. After all, I am a Conservative by nature. In spite of that, Obama's failure, in my view, with the *tax* question, coupled with his less than extraordinary stature concerned me greatly. Call me naïve, but I always felt that to be in the presence of a man qualified to become the President of the United States of America would feel like standing in the midst of greatness. Certainly, the mainstream media had built up this man's reputation as a titan among men. Maybe it's their fault for having set expectations so high, because I had anticipated that Obama's presence would have been so visceral that I could feel it. That simply wasn't the case with Obama, nor was it with McCain. Again, we'll get to the Senator from Arizona later.

Now, some of you are saying that I was out to set him up. Some, I have heard, suggest McCain put me up to this; that I was a "plant." This was echoed time and again by reporters, even amongst the mainstream media, whom we expect to better check their sources. However, it seems that far more of you are saying, "Yeah, finally someone has challenged this guy!" This goes for Obama supporters too, and I thank those of you who supported him and yet approached me on the street or wrote to me and applauded my actions.

Regardless of your preconceptions about this encounter, here are the facts: This was my neighborhood, and he interrupted my football game with my son. Moreover, I asked him a question that I believed then and still do now is valid—not just for me, but also for many across America that have similar aspirations to achieve the American Dream. Isn't that my right as an American? Isn't that my duty as an American? I respected Obama answering my questions. I appreciated his gracious and respectful demeanor towards me. Yet, not at any point during our discussion was I fooled. Like most of you, I know truth when I hear it. I know B.S. when I hear that too. Because I could care less about party loyalty, I know when a politician is giving me *straight talk* and when he or she is trying to feed me what I want to hear. In my view, Obama is a master at reading his audience and feeding them *red meat*.

My encounter with Obama ended affably. He most certainly realized that I was not among his core constituency, but was gracious about it. He did give me the impression, however, that he was in a sudden rush to leave the scene after our discussion. Perhaps he could sense that he had made an uncalculated error and that lingering would only add salt to the wound.

As Obama returned to his bus, I returned to my game of catch with my son. Neighbors returned to their homes, most of them Obama supporters at the time—and no, I was not attacked for my questioning of their candidate. My neighbors all know me, and regardless of politics, we care for one another. I'm there for them, just as they are for me. After all, at the end of the day we are all brothers and sisters and we are all Americans. Again, just ask any of them and they will tell you that I would have challenged McCain in the same manner if he had come down our street. That's just me. In fact, when given the chance on McCain's *Straight Talk Express*, I did indeed challenge him with a tough question. I'll share that engagement later on, as what transpired may surprise you.

So here's my question to you, regardless of which party you belong to or what political views you hold. What would you have done? What questions have you asked or are prepared to ask of your elected officials? I want Americans—everyday *Joes* and *Janes* to challenge our leaders. We put them in a place of authority to serve us, *We The People*. We must hold them accountable for their actions and judgments. We must demand more of their terms of service. You may not like the questions I asked of Obama, or what you will find out I asked of McCain, but you have to admit that more intense questioning of those we elect to positions of power is a good thing. If you want to know the real me, my fervent belief in the profound meaning of *Service* to our great country is a good place to start. It's not a Right or an Entitlement. It is a *Duty*.

2

Meeting the PRESS!!!

When Monday came around, it had all the appearance of a normal day-in-my-life. I was up at 4:30am, off to the gym at about five and back a couple of hours later to prepare Joey for school. After a quick breakfast and a hug goodbye from my boy, I jumped in the truck and headed off to work for the usual ten to twelve-hour workday. Before I got out the door, however, a friend of mine called me up from New Jersey and told me to check the Internet. He asked me to search "Obama and the Plumber." I remember typing in that search-phrase and finding something like eighty-one hits, but only half of them pertained to me. All the same, I had this silly grin on my face, thinking, *Hey, this is pretty cool. The Plumber and Obama.* Remember that I am a plumber. I wasn't used to any attention beyond a customer calling me about a leaky valve or a clogged drain line. Seeing a story about *me* on the Internet was pretty wild. Still, I thought little more of it and went to work. I didn't have the slightest expectation that anything else would develop and surely not the absolute madness that was about to strike.

Sometime during the day between muddy crawl spaces and leaking pipes under rotting cabinets, my phone rang. I can't remember exactly what time of day it was, only that the number was foreign to me. The caller ID showed the beginning area code of 210. *210?* At that time, it wasn't like me to ignore calls or screen them for over-zealous reporters. For all I knew, it might have been a customer using an out-of-state cell phone number or something. Regardless, I pushed the talk button and answered, "Joe here."

"Joe The Plumber?" questioned a young lady's voice.

"Uh yeah, this is Joe." My mind quickly shot back to that Inter-net search. *No way,* I thought.

"Hi Joe, I'm with KTSA News Radio 550 AM. We're a talk ra-dio station out of San Antonio, Texas. Could we get you to come on the air with us to talk about your question to Senator Obama yesterday?"

You have got to be kidding me? What do Texans care about what happened with a guy from Toledo, Ohio? I wondered how many folks out in San Antonio even knew there was a Toledo, Ohio on the map. No offense, it's just that Toledo ain't that exciting a place. It's home and I love it, but in terms of notoriety it's far from the likes of New York, Los Angeles or, for that matter, San Antonio.

I really didn't know what to say, so I awkwardly agreed, "Sure, why not."

With a notable measure of excitement, which struck me as odd, she said, "Thank you so much. Okay, hold on and we'll put you on the air in a moment."

"Okay, I'll be here," I replied, still not grasping their interest in me. *I'm just a plumber,* I kept saying to myself. Oh well, what the heck. If they wanted to talk with me, sure, why not? No harm in sharing my opinion. I had lots of experience in doing that. At any rate, I was more preoccupied with finishing up the job I was doing, because I had another appointment later that afternoon.

"Hey Joe?" She came back on the line a minute or two later.

"Yep, I'm here."

"Okay, we're going to put you on the air now," she advised.

A half-second later a man's polished radio voice came on the line. He was warm and excited to talk with me. His questions would be repeated by others for a solid week thereafter and continue even today. The thing that impressed me the most about the interview was how interested they were in me, a mere plumber. They were also very supportive, though I would not always find that to be the case amongst the media.

The rest of that day passed without further fanfare. I did kinda get a charge from that interview and shared it with my family that night. My dad subsequently took it upon himself to make a note on the refrigerator calendar—*Joe is a celebrity.*

Tuesday came quickly, as it usually does when you work such long days. The Wurzelbacher house followed the same routine as before; such as we did every day of the work and school week, but this day would ultimately foreshadow the absolutely mind-blowing events that were soon to come.

Right out of the gate that morning, the anvil was struck with a call from Fox News. It was another mystery area code, but this one was 212, which I would come to see often in the days ahead. As I came to understand, there are a great many media headquarters residing in New York City.

"Joe here."

"Hi, is this Joe—*Joe The Plumber?*" yet another young lady's voice asked.

"Yes . . ."

"Hi, I'm a producer at Fox News for *Your World with Neil Cavuto.* Would you be interested in calling into his show today? He'd like to speak with you about your encounter with Senator Obama this past weekend."

What's a Cavuto? "Uh sure," I replied, not knowing how to say no, and I still don't. Of course I knew of Fox News, but had never heard of a Neil Cavuto. I don't watch much television. Between work and raising my son, there is no time for it. Aside from that, she was grateful I had agreed to do the show and promised to call me back late that afternoon to plug me into the program.

As I hung up with her, I decided I had better find out who Cavuto was. If I was going to be on Fox News, chances were a great number of people were going to hear it, and I wanted to be prepared. Was this guy going to tear me up, or was he going to be supportive like the talk radio people? Yeah, I hear some of you. *Of course he was going to be supportive. It's Fox—the Conservative—News Channel.* All I can say is that not everyone at Fox sings my praise, which we'll get into later. For now, this was about Neil, who come to find out was something of a big-shot at Fox; anchor and managing editor of Fox Business News, a New York Times bestselling author, multiple award nominee and host of the #1 rated business show on television. I'm no media expert, but all that pretty much floored me. What could this guy possibly want to ask a *plumber?* Doesn't he already know it all?

Against my better judgment, I went forward with my commitment to do the show. Why not? They had asked politely and who was I to refuse. Again, this is just who I am.

Not long into the day, I began getting a number of other phone calls from yet more unrecognizable area codes. I can't begin to tell you where they all were from, except to say that it was radio. Yes, I would say it was a Fox News and talk radio tag-team effort that lit a fire under this story. Much like it had been with the San Antonio folks, all these talk radio hosts calling me were interested, energetically supportive and each politely commandeered only ten to fifteen minutes of my time. At first, I thought this was really cool. I had no idea so many folks, particularly in the media, shared my opinions. That said, I was quickly digging a deep hole in my workday.

When the Fox producer-lady called me back late that afternoon, she advised me about what to expect and then put me on hold until Neil was ready to patch me in. So, I waited patiently and listened to Mr. Cavuto wrap up his prior story and then set the stage for his interview of me by playing a couple of clips from my discussion with Obama.

Next thing I knew he announced my name, and I might add that he was able to pronounce Wur-zel-bach-er correctly—still can't understand why that has been so difficult for some in the media, particularly when they can pronounce names like Ahmadinejad just fine! Anyhow, Neil's first question came abruptly, "Joe, did he (Barack) win you over?"

It struck me as an odd question, because I didn't have the slightest impression of having been swayed by the senator's explanation of his tax plan. My response was unscripted and beholding to my core beliefs. I told Neil, "No . . . his answer even scared me more." Since I had not said anything of this nature to Barack, my response might have shocked some people, while possibly galvanizing others. I went on to explain to Neil that I thought Barack's plan was akin to socialism, that the Federal Government deciding how much money I should make, and how much of it should be redistributed to others was wrong. If you disagree with me, that's fine, but you are not being honest with others, and perhaps yourself, if you claim this is not a socialist ideal espoused by the likes of Karl Marx. Don't believe me? Here's the definition of *Socialism* right out of the Webster's dictionary:

SOCIALISM

1. any of various theories or systems of the ownership and operation of the <u>means of production and distribution</u> by <u>society or the community</u> rather than by private individuals, with all members of society or the community sharing in the work and the products. **2.** a) <u>political movement</u> for establishing such a system b) the doctrines, methods, etc. of the Socialist parties. **3.** the stage of society, in <u>Marxist doctrine</u>, coming between the capitalist stage and the <u>communist stage</u>, in which private ownership of the <u>means of production and the distribution</u> has been eliminated.

I will shred this concept to pieces later in the book, but the *means of production and distribution* is in fact **money**. The *society or the community* is the **government**; for example, the Soviet Union in Russia or the supposed People's Republic of China. This is a slippery slope folks, because Marx himself describes in his *Communist Manifesto* that socialism is the gateway to communism. Now do you understand why I was scared? If you still don't believe me, or you think I'm out in left field, look this stuff up for yourself.

Anyhow, Neil proceeded to ask me why I wasn't intimidated by Obama's gargantuan presence, how I felt about his *Robin Hood* persona and how his tax plan would affect me personally. Again, I just answered from my own personal viewpoints on these matters, as one who believes in following principle first and all else second. Barack's presence? Just didn't feel it, and it disappointed me. *Robin Hood?* Well, that guy stole from greedy rich nobles and gave to the peasants. Somehow, as an American citizen, I just don't see myself as a peasant, regardless of income bracket. Barack's tax plan benefiting me? That depends . . . I am hard-pressed to believe he won't wind up taxing us all to pay for his enormously expensive government entitlement programs in one way, shape or form. Moreover, I find it distasteful and morally reprehensible to take money away from someone who has worked harder than I have, been at it longer, or has had better breaks. In the Bible that's something called *Coveting*. Whether you are religious, you have to admit those Ten Commandments make a lot of common sense, because *coveting* your neighbor's wealth or property is destructive to oneself and society in general.

In closing, Neil said, "Joe, you're my kind of plumber." As it turns out, a great many in the country felt the same way. Today, I'm not sure if it was my meeting with Obama that sparked the media firestorm or those words from Neil.

I had hardly concluded Cavuto's interview when my phone really started hopping. It seemed like every media source in the entire country suddenly had my number! I conducted four or more radio interviews that evening and then had to work late into the night to get my jobs done for the day. Ouch, that was a long day . . .

No sooner did I walk in the door that night, well after supper, when Joey greeted me with excitement, "Dad, check this out!" They were all watching Fox News and he pointed to the scrolling text at the base of the screen.

Lo and behold, there was something about *Joe The Plumber* and *Barack Obama* and *Spreading The Wealth*. I could hardly believe it. I was too tired to believe it! What business did my name and profession have sharing the screen with a presidential candidate? Despite the gravitational pull of my bedroom, calling me to sleep, I instead succumbed to my curiosity and went to my computer to type in the search phrase *Barack Obama and Joe The Plumber*. The result was 371,000 hits! Can you believe that? I guess you probably can, considering all that transpired over the next several days.

The enormity of it hit me like a ton of bricks. I went from having slight amusement about a flicker of fame to absolute astonishment. Again, I got this stupid grin on my face and couldn't shake it off. I mean, what would you be thinking? I had the decidedly naïve notion that this might be good for business. However, nobody knew who *Joe The Plumber* was, except for my family and some close friends; oh, and Neil Cavuto, a Fox News producer and about a dozen or so talk radio stations all across the country. I sat there and thought for a moment. How exactly did all these guys compromise my cell phone number anyhow? I guess they were reporters and that was their job, but man, how fast were they.

Aside from all that, what really started to nag at me more than anything else was why a plumber could be so important in the grand scheme of the 2008 Presidential Election. That concept would bother me throughout the weeks that followed and still does today.

The Wurzelbacher house, for the most part, found it all rather amusing that night, but figured it would die out by the next day. Oh, how could we have been more wrong? I went to bed later than I had expected that night, trying to forget about my fifteen minutes of fame and refocusing my attention on the more relevant and pressing matters concerning a large job I had set up for Wednesday.

First thing the next morning, Governor Huckabee's producers at Fox News called me up. He had a weekend program at Fox, now that he was no longer a candidate, and he wanted me on the show. This was no call-in, however, they actually wanted to fly me out for the weekend, along with my dad and my son, which I thought was very cool. I had never been to New York before, and I had long desired to see Ground Zero to pay homage to those who had died there as a result of the 9-11 terrorist attacks. I had also been a supporter of Huckabee during the Republican Primaries, and thus looked forward to meeting him in person.

The folks at Fox were happy to ink me into their calendar, but later would be frustrated with me for giving so many other news organizations interviews before coming on Huckabee's program. Evidently, I had agreed to give them an *exclusive*, though I didn't recall having done so. Not that it mattered, because I was a plumber and didn't know what the heck an *exclusive* was! Diane Sawyer's people would later educate me. I know, sounds pretty wild, doesn't it.

From the beginning of that day and all throughout I never got one moment of rest from the media. Soon as I finished an interview, I got a call from another news organization or radio program wanting ". . . just five to ten minutes, really that's it . . ." Not that you need a reminder at this point in the story, but I just did not know how to say "No." Time and again I figured, *Sure, I can take a ten-minute break. No harm in that.* Also, being the opinionated person I am, I had occasionally called into a talk radio program or two to offer my opinion on whatever topic happened to stick in my craw. Now, for the first time ever in my life, here they were seeking my opinion, and in droves. Of course, my fascination with it quickly diminished when I realized the day was drawing swiftly to a close and I had a lot of unfinished work. A few ten-minute interviews are no problem. A couple dozen, with only a few minutes to spare in between, now that's a problem! Ultimately, it would take me another week of madness before I learned that setting a pace and sometimes saying, "No," was necessary for the sake of my sanity.

After another long and tiring 14-hour day, amidst countless media interview delays, I came home and congregated with my family before the television to watch the third and final presidential debate. My son Joey, mom and dad all wanted to talk about the growing *Joe The Plumber* phenomenon, but I wasn't having any of it. I really just wanted to watch the debate and then get some much needed sleep before I tried to catch up on job responsibilities the following day.

I remember having the sensation that this third and final debate was like the Super Bowl of debates. It was, by all accounts, McCain's last chance to appeal to the American people and catch up with Obama's seemingly runaway homestretch to the presidency. It was so important, in fact, that I decided to let my son stay up late that night to watch it. Just as my dad had instilled in me at a young age, I wanted Joey to experience the American political process and begin to develop an understanding of how and why our leaders are elected to their positions. He had watched the prior two debates, and we, the adults, had taken turns challenging him in a post-debate discussion to see just what he had learned from all he had seen and heard.

As you might have gathered by now, I inherently distrust politicians. By profession, they are masters of double-speak. You have to pay attention to really hear what they are saying, if and when they say anything at all. Notwithstanding, a politician is, at the least, saying something about his or her character. Such is why I wasn't merely satisfied to know that my son had watched the debate. I had to know if he was developing the B.S. litmus test skills that determine whether you become an individual as an adult or a drone.

When questioning him, I always ask my son for his thoughts first, before offering him my own. When I do get around to sharing my thoughts, I try not to interfere with his opinions. It is important to me that Joey develops his own points-of-view. After all, one day he will have to stand on his own two feet and have to explain, or at times defend, his positions. You can't stand on someone else's legs, unless of course you are not afraid of falling down.

The pre-debate news panels were just getting warmed up when someone knocked on our door. I got up to answer it and found a local television news camera crew waiting outside along with a reporter from the Toledo Blade newspaper. They politely asked if they could ask me a few questions and so I invited them in. This is how those pictures of me sitting pensively on my sofa watching the debate got out into the public. If you have seen those photos or get a chance to, notice that I am not frantically picking up phone call after phone call and that I am not surrounded by a dozen or more TV cameras. That madness was yet to come. At this point in the evening, it was just that local news crew, the newspaper guy and the Wurzelbachers awaiting the start of the debate. I answered a few questions, and then asked them to leave so we could watch the debate in privacy as a family. They really wanted to stay, but we didn't feel too comfortable with that idea, so out they went.

The debate began much in the same manner as the previous two—boring. I imagine that, like most folks, what we hope for in a Presidential Debate is a Heavyweight Title Bout, and yet what we always seem to get is a Tiddlywinks Tournament. Then suddenly I heard, "Joe The Plumber." Not a split second later my cell phone began ringing—a sound that did not cease for four solid weeks and will live on in infamy in my psyche. Hardly another moment went by when the television trumpeted out again, "Joe The Plumber," then again, "Joe The Plumber." At one point, I thought I was listening to a broken record. Again and again and again, both these guys were citing my name and profession like it was a new hip-hop single.

Meanwhile, my cell phone continued to ring and was joined by every other phone in the house in one great shrieking chorus. I couldn't tell where one call ended and the next one began. I had never heard anything like it in my life. The ringing was so incessant we couldn't hear the debate. We all tried answering the calls in hopes that we could satisfy the demand and move on, but it was useless trying to keep up. No matter how many media folks we spoke with or took messages from, a legion was waiting in line behind them. We probably shouldn't have answered any of the calls, hung up on them or disconnected the cord to the home phone and removed the batteries to the cell phones. Yet, once again, that would have been rude and we Wurzelbachers just don't abide rudeness. I'm now laughing at myself, just thinking about it. Albeit at the time, it wasn't very funny at all. My head was spinning, for I could hardly come to grips with what was happening. Somehow, beyond all rhyme or reason, I, Joe The Plumber, had become the focal point of a presidential debate. More than that, I was quickly becoming *the story* of the 2008 Presidential Election, an historic event all the talking suits on television agreed was the most important and pivotal of our lifetime. Holy Swing-Voter Batman!

So who were these camera and microphone-wielding minions storming the beaches of the Wurzelbachers' telecommunication lines? Just think of every name you have ever heard mentioned among the news media elite; Diane Sawyer, Katie Couric, Hannity and Colmes, Bill O'Reilly, and a swarm of others from all the alphabet soup stations; including, CNN, ABC, NBC, CBS, MSNBC, BBC—yes, even those from across the Atlantic and beyond. All this, because I had asked Obama a simple question?

Ultimately, phones can be dealt with, ignored or turned off if necessary. However, people at the door, on my front lawn and clogging my entire street with their news vans, trucks, trailers and satellite vehicles was absolutely nuts. How does one ignore knocking at your door without end? You don't. You open it and get barraged by reporters armed with pens, papers, microphones, recorders, cameras, lights and portable x-ray machines (okay, that last one is an exaggeration). Nonetheless, it was a scene straight out of the movies. They were fighting for position in my tiny front doorway, shouting over each other with questions, "Joe! Hey Joe! One question Joe!" I hardly knew where to begin to answer them. How did they find my house so fast? Really, it was unbelievable. It was like everyone in the world, besides my family and I, knew what was going to happen in that debate and had a GPS homing beacon positioned on my rooftop. Heck, the debate hadn't concluded yet!

Finally, I heard a coherent question from among the platoon of reporters, "Joe, how does it feel to be mentioned in the debate?"

I barely opened my mouth to speak when another question was shot my way, "Hey Joe, now you've been mentioned 14 times." Another moment went by and I heard, "Hey Joe, now you've been mentioned 20 times . . . 22 times . . ." The crazy thing was, the media were keeping pace with the debate and I couldn't, because I was too busy trying to answer phone calls and their questions at the door. I'm not exactly sure how many times I was mentioned in the debate, and I don't much care. All I know is that a train left the station that night and that the real Joe The Plumber was on it. He left me at the station holding the bag, without a ticket, without a pocketbook and without a destination.

At some point that night I remember getting a call from Katie Couric, yep that little-known journalist from the CBS Evening News. She asked if she could interview me and I naturally obliged. Meanwhile, my dad had Diane Sawyer on the other line, vying for an *exclusive* the following morning for her show, Good Morning America.

I thought Katie was pretty cool, despite her mispronunciation of my name, which she later corrected. She asked me how I had met the candidates, and my honest response somehow labeled me a racist the following day. I was describing how I came to meet Obama in my neighborhood and that I wanted to ask him a tough question. I then said that I thought he tap-danced around my question, *"Almost as good as Sammy Davis Junior."* Uh oh, I compared Obama with a black performer, so I must be a racist. Good grief! I could hear Katie and her crew chuckling at my comment on their end. Are they racists too? Some extremist nut-jobs might say so, and that is sad. Truthfully, Sammy Davis was one of my favorite performers. How exactly does that reconcile with racism?

After concluding my interview with Katie, I then got on the phone with Diane Sawyer, or rather the lady that turned out to be her producer. I guess Diane wasn't able to hang on the line any longer. Her producer, however, politely explained to me what an *exclusive* was and asked if I would be so kind as to grant her one. From my amateur understanding, an *exclusive* meant that I couldn't give another news organization or reporter an interview for four hours after Diane. That sounded all right by me. I figured I could use a breather from ALL the media, and agreed.

I finally shut my front door that night and went to my room to seek council from up on High. Perhaps the toughest thing to deal with that night was getting my thirteen-year-old son to go to bed for school amidst all the excitement over his dad. Thinking of my son and the effect all this nonsense might have on him, I prayed for wisdom. I prayed for guidance and understanding. I prayed that this happening in my life would not stray me from the righteous path I had taken many years ago, a path that had seen me reunited with my son. Nothing in the world comes anywhere near to my love for Joey and my sense of duty as a father.

Sometime during the night, the police showed up to clear the media juggernaut off the street, or at least reorganize their campsite to allow for the garbage pickup due the next morning. I found it difficult to sleep, and really wouldn't sleep soundly again for nearly three weeks. At about 3:30am, someone started hammering at my door. I jumped up and ran to the front door and opened it to see what the emergency was. Another reporter! I read him the riot act and slammed the door shut. This was a home, my home, not a news studio. My mom had to get up in an hour to go to work and my son needed his rest for school that day. Had they no respect? No, many of them did not.

Instead of trying to go back to sleep for another hour, I decided to click on the TV and see if I could find a rerun of the debate. I did, and finally got to sit and watch it without interruption. I still couldn't believe they were talking about me. It really felt like they were talking about another guy named Joe, or an abstract plumber who served each of their independent visions for what the real working class in this country wanted in a president. By the end of the debate, I had seen the exact opposite of what I had hoped to find. Neither candidate had said or done anything to sway me in his direction. It was all just another political say-nothing sparring session.

It was still dark when I headed out for the gym for a much needed workout. Thankfully, I was unobstructed by media. Despite the 3:30am incident, perhaps it was too early in the morning for most of the regular news, and I enjoyed having some quiet time out of the house to reflect on all that had happened. In hindsight I suppose I should have been thinking more about what was ahead, but I was still under this illusion that this frenzy over Joe The Plumber would soon die out.

At the gym I had a good run on the treadmill, during which I contemplated my upcoming interview with Diane Sawyer. *Are you kidding me?* What was I going to say? What more did I have to say? It really was a simple question that I had asked Obama. How many more ways did I have to spell it out?

At any rate, as I thought about the interview, my schedule came to mind. It was going to be tight this morning, juggling getting Joey off to school and then there was work. I had a full day ahead of me and I prayed I wouldn't be interrupted. My poor boss had to have been losing his patience by now.

As I hit the weights, I retraced the events of the night before and the days before that, all the way back to my having met Obama. It was just wild. In between sets I would burst out in an impulsive fit of laughter. I couldn't contain it. The more I thought about what had happened, the more I laughed. People near me must have thought I was losing my mind. Then it happened. I began to realize that my anonymity might have been compromised. I started looking out of the corners of my eyes, wondering how many of those working out next to me knew who I was. Everywhere I looked, I saw eyes staring at me and folks whispering to each other. It honestly made me nervous. Were they going to be angry with me? Was I going to be yelled at? Attacked? I really didn't know what to expect. The answer came as I made my way towards the exit and a lady stopped me. "You're Joe The Plumber," she said.

"Shhh . . ." I gave her a sheepish grin.

It was too late, for others overheard her and before I knew what was happening the entire gym had migrated over and surrounded me. Now I was really nervous. Then the most surprising thing happened. I saw smiles and heads nodding approvingly, and they gave me a standing ovation. One after another, they told me how much they appreciated my having asked the question, that they respected my having spoken up and really took heart that someone had stuck up for them. I'm someone who keeps to himself, so I really didn't know any of these folks, and yet we all had somehow formed a bond. I wasn't sure what to make of it, except that it was moving and it was real.

Believe it or not, when I returned home from the gym the crowd of reporters and news vehicles had grown larger from the night before. I had to park at my neighbor's house, because I couldn't get to mine. I uncomfortably burrowed my way through the various reporters, assailing me with questions, to my door. I had to meet with Diane Sawyer soon, with whom I had agreed to an *exclusive*. Ha ha ha, sorry folks, but I have a four-hour irrevocable liberty pass. Personally, I thought this had been one of my wiser decisions of late. The idea of not having to answer any questions for four hours felt like a vacation in the Bahamas. This meant that all the rest of the media had to honor my commitment and lay off, right? Wrong . . . In fact, every single one of them exhaustively tried to convince me of how an *exclusive* was not really an *exclusive* after all. Is there no honor amongst thieves?

Back inside my house and away from peppering questions, I made breakfast, helped Joey get prepared for school and then prepared to greet Good Morning America. It was a short trip out to my front yard, which had been miraculously transformed into a sound-studio, complete with lighting effects and my very own beanbag (my standing position for the shoot). Beneath the glory of blaring camera lights, a team of techno-cyborgs (production assistants) swiftly took me by each arm and directed my way towards the *beanbag*. Another team of cyborg production assistants immediately encroached my personal spaces, fitting me with all sorts of batteries and gadgets to plug me in for the interview. I call them cyborgs, because they had these headsets and constantly jabbered back and forth with whom I presumed were the network folks back at headquarters, doing sound checks and whatever else those people do. Half the time, I couldn't tell if they were talking to me or the voice in their ear. Either way, let's just say it was an uncomfortable experience. I'm used to meeting people, shaking their hand and getting to know them before they get to poke and prod me in certain areas.

After completing a couple of mic checks I stood patiently in the *beanbag* position for what seemed like an eternity, waiting to hear the voice of Diane Sawyer. Again, I have to laugh at myself. Me and Diane? Hah! As the moment neared to address Good Morning America's national audience—LIVE—I began to get a little nervous. I hadn't thought too much about these interview moments before, but this wasn't as simple as talking with someone over the phone. I was going to be seen and my words would be heard all across the country. I decided I had better bow my head and ask God to not let me trip over my tongue, and that I might make my family and friends proud.

When the camera turned on and Diane asked the first question, a feeling of calm swept over me and I felt comfortable throughout the interview. As with Katie the night before, I did get the sense that it was hard for Diane to understand why a guy like me, far from rich, didn't want *the rich* kicking over some of their hard-earned dollars to me. Again, I had to call out the socialist concept of redistributing wealth. She also fixated on my voting preference for the election, as if there was much of a question in anyone's mind. Then she asked a question that struck me as odd at the time. Was I registered to vote? Little did I know the smear campaign against me had already begun. At least she pronounced my last name correctly, as opposed to McCain's "Wurtzel-berger" mishit in the debate. Altogether, her interview was fair and, like Katie, she was pleasant to speak with.

Upon completing the interview and being disconnected by the cyborgs from ABC, I checked in with my son, who was really digging the whole experience. After all, his dad was *Joe The Plumber*. I was looking forward to my four hours of respite from the media, but it was not to be. No sooner had I left the ABC studio in my yard than I was hounded by Camp Reporterville. I tried to explain to them, again, that I had given Diane an *exclusive* and I wasn't about to break my word, so they would have to wait until 11am. In spite of that, their universal response was, "That's okay, this is local."

As a media outsider, I really did not understand the rules about such things, but I wasn't buying their story. I did admire their persistence, however, so I told them, "Here's my son, his best friend and his little sister. You can interview them for now."

The press mob jumped on it, and I wasn't surprised at this point. I figured they would have interrogated my garbage man if he had made the mistake of pausing too long while picking up my trash. My son loved it, and I hope he will cherish that moment, but also understand exactly what it all meant.

The phones never stopped ringing throughout that day and the next four weeks. In fact, the media abuse caused a meltdown in one of my cell phones before the day had gotten started. At one point, I bought a new phone with a new number, just so I could have a phone that didn't ring all the time. It didn't take long for that number to be compromised as well. In retrospect, I probably should have just lived without a phone for the next few weeks and left the country, perhaps on a fishing trip to Alaska. Yeah, that would have been real nice. Had I known what the next two days would bring, I would have done just that.

3

I Really Am A Plumber

It wasn't more than twenty-four hours after the debate when the invasion of my privacy began. I have no doubt about the intentions of those who pursued such information and what they hoped to accomplish by exposing every minute detail about my personal life. These attacks were malicious and deliberate in their attempt to ruin me, my pursuits and to damage and defame my family. They must have believed that their nefarious efforts would succeed in discrediting me and silencing my voice. Their intended effect had just the opposite results. I would have been content to let my fifteen minutes of fame die out and fade back into anonymity. However, what they did to my family and me could not go unanswered. It's a matter of right and wrong, and I have always believed in the words of Edmund Burke, the great British Conservative who supported the American colonists prior to the revolution. He said, *"All that is necessary for the triumph of evil in America is for good men to do nothing."*

Late Thursday morning after Good Morning America and the stupefying swarm of news media (domestic and foreign), a reporter for the Toledo Blade came to my house accompanied by the now usual media cohort of reporters and cameramen. He was pleasant enough, and yet he seemed to have an agenda. He asked me a series of simple innocuous questions about my encounter with Barack, the debate, and my career as a plumber . . . I should have smelled something coming, but out came the knife before I knew what struck me. He asked if I was a licensed plumber. His question was pointed and carried with it a sense of arrogant invasiveness.

I took this reporter, who was now behaving more like a lawyer, into my house and asked him if we could speak "off the record." He shrugged as if he didn't know what I was talking about. Since having learned a long series of hard lessons as a child, I proceeded to tell him the only thing I knew to tell a person anymore. I told him the truth, "No." I also explained, however, that my boss was a licensed Master Plumber, and that the city and county permitted me to work under his license and supervision. Unfortunately, that fell on deaf ears, and I quickly realized the crosshairs that had been painted on my big forehead. I asked him, "Do you know you are messing with my life?"

With a smug expression he asked, "What do you mean?"

I tried to politely explain to this newspaper guy that if this were his family, or job, or livelihood that was being messed with, he would show some discretion, or at least some restraint.

The reporter from the Blade did not remotely care. The story, or perhaps ruining my reputation was more important. Instead of him saying, "Hey man, I hear ya. This really has nothing to do with the election anyhow, so I'll make sure we don't print something that endangers your career or worse." Nope, he threw up his hands and instead responded, "The people have a right to know. It's out of my hands."

I should have asked him if he and his buddies throughout the media kept score when they ruined people's lives. You hear about it once in a while, when the media happens to report the impact they have on someone's life. Living it is altogether different and the punishment is real.

It wasn't long into the day when an article was posted on the Blade's website and then in the next day's paper about how I wasn't a plumber after all, or at least I wasn't a "licensed plumber." Get the picture? The rest of the article aside, that opening line set the stage for a rash of Internet blogs that regurgitated this insane notion that I wasn't a plumber, but was a McCain plant, sent to seek out Obama at one of his rallies. Yeah . . .

That Blade article went on to assert that I was an unlicensed, untrained and ultimately unqualified plumber. The tone of the piece pretty much painted a picture of me, day in and day out, screwing up people's houses with my work. Instead of asking other plumbing companies and plumbers in the area to corroborate my explanation, or to find out that my situation was common in the area and throughout the county, they went to the local head of the United Association of Plumbers, Steamfitters and Service Mechanics to discredit me. What was their beef? Aside from having zero knowledge about me personally or professionally, one can only imagine, but I'm pretty sure their public endorsement of Obama had something to do with it. Perhaps they were also sore that I had not joined their union. Regardless of their opinion about me, their spokesperson deliberately and aggressively cast aspersions about my plumbing qualifications that were absolutely false and misleading.

According to the Toledo Blade's article, a certain business manager for the union, who I have decided not to name for the sake of his family, said, *"This individual has got no schooling, no licenses, he's never been to a training program, union or non-union, in the United States of America."*

So when did Texas and Alaska, where I was trained by the military and by local Master Plumbers cease to be a part of the USA? Are those states too big or too far in the South or the North? I probably should give the guy a break. Maybe he missed school the day they covered that subject.

Nevertheless, after talking with that Toledo Blade reporter, I closed my door and spoke with no more press. It wasn't amusing anymore, nor was it time to be polite and affable.

I got another call from my friend in New Jersey, with whom I had been stationed in Alaska. He told me to get to the computer and look up some of the blogs and reports out on me. I couldn't believe it. About every crazy thing you could imagine was being said about me. The first accusation was easy to digest, as supposedly I wasn't a plumber. Hmm, where could that have come from? But then it got a lot more personal, and downright mean. Come to find out, I was indeed a McCain plant at an Obama rally, a registered Republican *(Oh No!)*, a tax-evader, not registered to vote (they must have been confused), a member of the Keating Five (whatever that meant), a racist, a wife-beater and a deadbeat dad. Those last three really got me steamed up. I just couldn't believe the gall of these people, spreading such wicked lies against someone about whom they clearly didn't know the first thing. Have they no shame? Clearly, they do not.

My friend, hearing nothing but the seething silence on my end of the phone asked in a worried voice, "What are you going to do? Maybe you should stop, Joe."

I didn't know what to say. I was frozen to the core. I started looking around the room and got up to walk around the house, circling myself repeatedly. I was looking at the lights on in the bathroom and hallway. I thought about my minutes on my cell phone, the expense of the Internet connection that allowed me to browse the filth being spread about me. I might lose my job. How was I going to pay for all those bills piled up on my desk, keep my house and buy groceries? How was I going to support Joey and would I lose him? It took nine hard and pride-swallowing years of my life to get him back, to have the opportunity to be his father and see him raised into the man I always dreamt he'd be. God help me if I lost him. He was the entire meaning of my life and I realized I might have just endangered all the blessings that he meant to me by opening my big mouth. How in the world was I going to undue what had been done, so I could go back to being a simple plumber and a father to my son?

With legions of press hounding my every step, I had to call my boss and tell him I couldn't make it to work that day. I also told him about the Blade reporter and apologized for any trouble it might cause him. That day was one of the darkest in my life. I did the best

I could to hide my concerns from my parents and my son, but in reality I was despondent. I didn't know how I was going to get out of this mess. I had just gotten beyond living paycheck to paycheck and had set only a little money aside for a rainy day, which evidently had come. I also had recently moved my parents in with me to help them out in a time of need. My father has a medical condition and cannot work. So, you see, it wasn't just Joey I was working to provide for, it was practically my entire family.

That evening, I split my time between the television, watching the negative news reports on me and browsing the Internet trash machines of the Huffington Post, the Daily Kos and others. I just couldn't understand why *a plumber* was so dang important amidst *the most important election of our lifetime.* What was wrong with these people? What was wrong with Obama and McCain? Couldn't they all find some more important issues to talk about?

So let me pause for a minute or two from my moments of despair and let me address some of these myths about me. First, I am and have long been a plumber. Truth is, I have done few other things in my professional life. When I was a boy, the most influential male role model in my life, aside from my dad, was my Uncle Doug. He was in fact a Master Plumber. After graduating from high school as a JROTC Major I enlisted in the Air Force to serve my country and to become a Crew Chief, a mechanic of sorts servicing F-16 Fighting Falcons. That would have been THE COOLEST JOB, but for better or worse, after I survived boot camp I was informed that the USAF was full up on Crew Chiefs. I had four basic options for tech school, HVAC, Electrical, Carpentry or Plumbing. You might be asking yourself, don't they need pilots in the Air Force. The answer is yes, and I could have qualified with my twenty-fifteen vision, in fact that is the kind of quality they look for in pilots. However, they are not particularly looking for pilots who have a MAJOR problem flying. Yes, I have this funny thing about heights and gravity. So, what were my choices again? Oh yes, I was already an adept carpenter, HVAC didn't interest me and electrical just plain scares me. As a plumber, you might frequently get wet, which is something I am plenty ready to suffer next to getting shocked and killed! Alas, Joe the United States Air Force Plumber it was.

Courtesy of the United States Air Force, I was on my way to plumbing school at Shepherd Air Force Base in Wichita Falls, Texas. They put me through a comprehensive training course, from which I graduated. I reckon that shows the true color of our local United Association of Plumbers, Steamfitters and Service Mechanics' spokesman, and says something about the quality and accuracy of The Toledo Blade's reporting. Anyhow, I digress . . .

After the United States Air Force deemed me fit to be a plumber, I was asked to provide my top three choices for station assignments. At the top of my list was Alaska. It may sound odd to some, but I wanted an Alaska assignment something fierce. I had dreamed about the famed last bastion of the North American frontier ever since I first read one of my all-time favorite books, *The Call of the Wild,* by Jack London. I was only eight years old at the time, but the vivid portrait of pristine beauty, isolation and wildlife untamed by city limits, highways, dams and bridges totally captivated my imagination. You had to be a real man to live there. Death was certain for those who weren't tough enough or couldn't learn to survive under the brutal rules of the land and the elements.

Whether by virtue of chance, timing or the simple fact that the Air Force could hardly find anyone crazy enough to want to be a plumber in the bone-chilling subzero temperatures of Alaska, I was granted the post of my dreams. I will share more about this experience later in the book, but let me tell you something about plumbing in Alaska. I absolutely loved it!

With the plumber question settled, let us discuss this insanity about my relation to Charles Keating and the "Keating Five"? Are you kidding me? What the heck is the "Keating Five"? I guess since I bear the last-name of Wurzelbacher, I'm immediately related to all the other Wurzelbachers in the country, and in particular those who may have skeletons in their closets. Yep, I chalk this one up to the Major Leagues of B.S.

What else was cast out there to denigrate my reputation, to ruin my career, and ultimately to shut me up? Well, I'm evidently a racist, because I said Obama tap-danced around my questions with about as much skill as Sammy Davis Jr. Fact is, I love Sammy Davis Jr., and I only used him as an analogy for lack of a better tap-dancer coming to mind. Oh yes, I'm also a wife-beater, which really floored me. Ask anyone who knows me and they will tell you that I believe there is a special place in hell for men who abuse women. It is personal to me, and I would not and could not become something I despise practically above all else. Deadbeat Dad? Yep that's me, the single father raising my son, who incidentally lives with me fulltime. Plumber without a license? Answered. Tax-evader? Again, answered. I had been working very hard to pay off my tax and other debt, that is, until the media and Liberal smear-merchants attacked me and put my employer's small business OUT OF BUSINESS!

Did I ever say I made $250,000 a year or more? NO. Did Obama and Biden play that idea up in speeches and with the media? YES. Why? I reckon they just couldn't understand why a guy like me, a bona fide member of the middle-class and all, wouldn't embrace *Robin Hooding* my neighbor who has a few more bucks than I do. Didn't Obama get a good look at my house when he visited my street? Didn't the media, in all those days camped out on my doorstep? Oh yeah, I forgot that I was also a McCain plant that went to Obama's rally.

Not long ago, I did an interview for one of the primetime news programs. The anchor, a polished and sophisticated female reporter, whose suit probably cost more than my house, asked her first question, "So Joe, when the McCain campaign contacted you and sent you out to that Obama rally to ask the now famous question about his tax plan . . ."

I nearly got up and left the interview right then. "What rally?" I questioned, but really felt like screaming at that point. Haven't you seen the footage? Did it look to you like we were in a football stadium? Did you see any Greek Columns in the background? Lord give me strength. She didn't bat an eyelash or belie any expression whatsoever. She went right on asking me questions almost like she didn't hear a word I said. It was like she had been poisoned by the media-Borg, programmed to believe what the Left had told her, or maybe she was just determined to tell the story she wanted her viewers to hear. It's not in my nature to be rude, so I stayed put and politely answered all of her questions as plain as I could. If it is truly their intent to be accurate, then how can they, the media, be so poorly informed.

In all, the attacks that hurt the most were those that cost me my job, put my boss out of business and infected my family with a sense of insecurity in our otherwise safe and secure home. The minions of the Democrat political machine mobilized a successful campaign against me, a private citizen, which stirred up hatred you cannot believe. Some of the things that were written to me are so vile, I had to take extra care to make sure my son wouldn't discover them. They also came after my employer's plumbing company, harassed our customers and went out of their way to stir up claims of plumbing malpractice. Fact was, we were among the best of the best. We lived by referral and stood tall and proud upon the quality and professionalism of our work. I don't mind saying that when my boss told me he had to close up shop, I had an identity crisis. The world—and I do mean the world, crazy as that sounds—knew me as Joe The Plumber, but in reality, I was Joe the Unemployed.

So why continue to speak out, in spite of the advice of friends and family? Why didn't I shrink out of sight, find a nice tight crawlspace under a house to slink into, or hop a plane to Fiji or some other far corner of the world? Well, for one I couldn't afford a plane ticket to nowhere if they were giving them away for free. I was broke! Yet, in all seriousness, it was my sense of civic duty and the fighting American spirit within me that wouldn't let me give in. I could not let them win, scare me off or shut me up. Had I done so, what would that have said to all the Middle Americans across the country who were watching my story unfold? It would have sent a clear message to all to beware the power of the politician. Dare not challenge the might of the media. They are stronger and more fearsome than we, and we are but average and insignificant. Woe unto he or she that dares to cross them!

Some have claimed, whether Conservative or Liberal, that I crave the media spotlight and that I live for the attention. As I have said repeatedly, I am a private kind of guy—more private than most. This better part of this experience has been about as uncomfortable as anything I could have imagined. Having every detail of my background, my finances, my driving records and virtually every thing worth knowing about me jerked out into the open for public consumption is like those dreams we all have of finding ourselves naked in a classroom amongst our peers. No, I surely do not like anything about the supposed limelight in the slightest. Nonetheless, God gave me the spirit to fight. He made me stubborn. He made me to be the type of person who doesn't back down, and to stand taller when the flack gets hotter and louder. Some of you who have supported me throughout all this have said I was just the right man for the job, but I'm just Joe. It is too late for me to change now.

The thing that has been most gratifying came initially as a surprise to me, but has since given new meaning to my life. It is the support of all of you that has sustained me; your letters, your phone calls, our chance meetings around the corner and down the street. You have called me out in New York, Philadelphia and all across Ohio. You have reached out to me from every corner of our great country. I have even been approached by folks from countries I could not believe would have an interest in me; countries like Great Britain, Pakistan, Czechoslovakia, South Africa, Spain, France, Italy and Australia. What I did in the days that followed was not for me. It was for Joey, for my parents, for all my friends and family, my neighbors and for you. You may be among those who wanted to see me disappear, but I hope you will change your mind about my intentions by the time you finish reading this book.

I am not special, nor do I believe I have a calling or that I have some self-image of greatness to protect. I do what I believe the Lord would have me do. It's just that simple. What challenges I faced in the days and weeks ahead were hard. Truly, you have no idea. I wanted nothing more than to disappear and take one of the many jobs offered to me from across the country and in my own hometown. Still, that would not have set an example for my son, for whom I pray our country will remain strong and free. I dare say it would not have set a good example for those of you who might have an opportunity in the future to question one of our elected officials. Regardless of your political leanings, I want you to protect and exercise that Right. The moment we give up on it and rely upon opposing parties or the media to ask all the tough questions, or simple questions like mine, we're through. The greatness of our nation can more easily be undone than you might expect. Many great nations in history have unraveled before and it will happen again. What I witnessed in the days and weeks ahead only reinforced my view of how fragile our freedom is.

4

Hard Lessons Are The Best

Let me say that if you are among the crowd that thought I was making a ton of money with the fame thrust upon me, or figured this experience was like going to Disney World, or thought the Republican Party was paying me a fortune to stick my neck out, then you either haven't been paying attention or you have only gotten your information from the *Choir News*.

Who or what is the *Choir News?* I suppose that depends on which side of the political pendulum you swing. I don't care how much a news organization or personality claims to be impartial and balanced, you have to remember that you are dealing with people. People, by their very nature, are opinionated. Only a robot wouldn't inject their personal bias into a job that requires reporting of issues that are polarizing.

Wherever you got your information, or from whatever basis you formed your opinion about my situation, understand that I was and still am flat broke. I had a job and was pulling myself out of debt, but you already know how that went. I decided to do a book, but as you may have heard, I went with a small publisher to make a point about supporting small business and passed up on an opportunity for a fat advance. Should I have my head examined? Maybe, but I think everything will work out in the end. I have learned a great many lessons in life, hard lessons that have taught me a system of values that I am determined not to compromise. How hard were they? Let's just say they are the kinds of things for which many people spend fortunes on therapists to help sort out. As for me, I'm grateful for every one of them. I honestly wouldn't change a thing if given the opportunity for an easier life. Why? Because hard lessons are the best way to build up your internal strength, a fortified spirit and the wisdom and will to achieve success.

What I am about to share with you will explain, in some measure, what I believe makes up the fabric of our country and why I chose the course I did during the final days of the 2008 election. I sought and realized no monetary gain, but all the personal reward one could ask for. Despite my fears about the consequences of fighting on, I challenged myself to follow what I believed was my civic duty.

I have an uncanny memory of my childhood. I can remember pieces of it from the time I was two years old. The first lesson I can remember learning early on is that work, and often hard work, is both necessary and good for the soul. From my earliest childhood memories I was impressed by the measure of my family's dedication to a tireless work ethic. Aunts, uncles, grandparents and all shared the same creed.

When you are poor, and you need to repair or build something, you can't just pick up the phone and call the local contractor, get an estimate, put them to work and do nothing more strenuous than write out a check. I know many of you can relate to this, but when I was growing up, there were many weeks when we barely had enough money for groceries, let alone the cost of a repairman. So, when something went wrong around the house or with the car, we were pretty much out of luck. We had to learn how to do things for ourselves and find the extra time to do it, or we lived without the basic necessities we Americans commonly take for granted these days. Take plumbing, for example, and imagine your water heater breaks in the dead of winter. You have three choices; spend about five hundred bucks to have a new one installed, attempt to fix it yourself or take ice-cold showers until the arrival of summer, at which time they will just be cold showers without the ice. I know there are many of you for whom an expense of five hundred dollars right now is just not an option. In that boat we sit together.

In the face of such struggles, this is where the heart and soul of our country, the Middle-Class—Our Class, is the strongest. Growing up, there was hardly ever a week that went by without a family project in the hopper. In the absence of having that five hundred bucks lying around, we poured concrete, built houses, fixed cars, and repaired plumbing. We did it as a family, or with neighbors and friends. We came together for each other, not because of guilt or debt or because it was expected. No one kept score to see whose turn it was to pitch in or who was in line next for the help. We supported each other because that was who we were, and it felt good. In helping each other we found a sense of accomplishment that went far beyond anything we could do for wages. Our labor, our sweat and the product of our efforts were our own. No one could put it on a shelf and sell it away for a pittance of the value of the labor that went into it. No corporation could fire the help we gave one another and no government could tell us to give it away to someone in the next county or state or country. Do you get the point? This is what freedom is all about in America.

If your family or community was anything like mine, then you worked hard and you played hard. The harder the work, the harder and the more gratifying the play became. Mostly, we would have our Sabbath every Sunday after church. Family friends and all would migrate to Rocky Bayou State Park in Florida's panhandle. Us kids would go swimming and water skiing, while the adults visited and rested from a long week of hard and productive labor. These were good times, and wouldn't nearly have had the same meaning if we had spent the week sitting around on our butts doing nothing.

Another lesson I learned that went hand in hand with hard work was pride. My grandfather had a home-based business for most of his life. His specialty was working with concrete. He would work on people's foundations, patios, steps and made all sorts of concrete forms for various household and outdoor items; like flower boxes, birdbaths, statuettes and pretty much any concrete item you would find in the big hardware store chains today. He was a master of his trade and prided himself on it. The larger and more established builders and contractors would often come to him for tips and training in his craft, because he was widely known for the quality of his work. One of his trademarks was that his molds never broke. He was an absolute perfectionist and had survived hard times during the Great Depression because of his quality workmanship and tireless dedication to those for whom he worked. He used to tell me, "Joe, I'm the best at what I do, because I care. When I work on someone's home or make something for someone to take home, I look at it like it is my own." He was a part of the rare breed of American that built the foundation of our country. There was hardly anything he couldn't do. He built his own house as well as others. In addition to concrete work, he was an adept carpenter, plumber, and electrician. I guess he wasn't able to pass the latter onto me.

Despite all the great examples I had in my life of hard work, ethics, dedication and taking pride in one's work, at the tip of the hardworking spear was my mother. Before she met my dad she worked three jobs to provide for my brother and I. I never saw her complain and, God bless her, she never seemed to tire. One might wonder when she ever found time to raise my brother and I between punching time-clocks and getting the minimal amount of rest one needs just to function. Nevertheless, she always made time for us. We were taught morals, values and the meaning of love. About once a week she would take Bobby and I to Lincoln Park near where we lived in Valparaiso, next to Eglin Air Force Base. My brother and I would go swimming and she would stand on the shoreline just smiling from ear to ear, as though she didn't have a care in the world. Her love for us was ironclad and you could feel it from across the park just as well as you could in her embrace. On our way home from the park, we always used to pass by this old plantation-style hotel. Despite its age and dilapidated state, you could tell it was once a gem. "Mom," I always said as we passed by the place, "one day I'm gonna buy you that place, and I'm gonna fix it up real nice for you." I have never forgotten it, and I still hope that one day I can buy it for her and fulfill those many promises.

Naturally, with mom working so often, I learned early on to step up and carry my weight around the home. I was cleaning house and cooking dinner by the time I was eight. I realize some of you might find that tragic, but I was happy to, and I know many of you also had to carry some of the household burden at a young age. Frankly, I think it was a good thing, and I believe we would all be better off if there were more of that kind of responsibility being instilled in our youth these days. Working hard and learning how to be responsible for something beyond oneself at a young age builds character. Particularly in this country, I believe that the earlier in life you begin to build character, the stronger it will be when you become an adult and have the power to affect the lives of others with your vote. Think about that for a moment. What sort of basis will so many children today being raised by daycare, nourished by fast-food and TV-dinners, and educated by X-box have when they reach voting age? How many kids these days even understand the meaning of the voting right they have inherited by the genius of our forefathers and the blood of patriots?

Another tough lesson I learned early on in life was standing up against something or someone much stronger than yourself. Let's just say that my first father wasn't great, and he didn't treat my mom all that well. He had a problem with the drink and with his ensuing temper. Twice before I turned four, I stood up to him in defense of my mother. I paid a price, but I wouldn't give up and never regretted it. I was a young boy who loved his mother and wanted to protect her. What son doesn't?

Despite the abuse, my Mom did her best to keep the family to-gether and her husband's rage under control. Yet, it wasn't meant to work out, and I thank God for that. When I was five, we decided to go on a rare vacation getaway and went to Disney World. As a boy, I would often get bloody noses for no reason at all. It just so happened that during our tour of Disney World, one of my nostrils began to bleed. Angered by this, the man who was supposed to protect and care for me, decided to bloody the other nostril. Why? Who in their right mind could say?

It wasn't long after we returned home from our family vacation that he ran off with another woman and abandoned his wife and two sons with a pile of debt and unsavory debt collectors. I can still remember a biker gang arriving at my house and accosting my mother, demanding she tell them where he had gone. Evidently, he owed them a fair sum of money and they aimed to collect. Unfortunately, they didn't believe my mom when she told them he had run off. Rather than come back another day or look elsewhere, these vermin decided to ride their bikes right through our front door. They tore up our house, then rode out back and destroyed our above-ground pool, before finally deciding my mom was telling them the truth.

After that incident, my mom sat both my brother Bobby and I down to explain to us that our father wasn't coming home ever again. I can still hear her voice as it was that night, "Boys, he won't be coming back."

Bobby was too young to understand it, and doesn't recall much of it today. As for me, I initially felt an overwhelming sense of relief that the horror had at last gone and would not return. It felt like peace, something I had never known. Still, that innate connection a child has with his parent settled in, and I realized that although I didn't want my father, I did indeed want and need *a father*. "Why?" I had managed to ask my mom, not truly understanding what I was asking. Perhaps I was asking larger questions, such as, *Why this was our family? Why did we have to have a dad like him?*

It wasn't long thereafter that I fell into a deep despair. Here I was, a five-year-old boy, hardly more than a toddler and I had become suicidal. I decided one day to dig a grave in the backyard.

When my mom arrived home from work that evening, I showed it to her and asked that she bury me in it. I feel awful for putting her through the absolute devastating emotions that must have seized her heart that day. But I was only five. I didn't know how else to deal with my grief and longing for the vision I had of a true father.

Like I said, hard lessons, and yes, they are the best. I admit that I would not want the worst of my childhood for my son, or yours. However, those occurrences, as terrible as they were, gave me the inner strength I have today. They also fortified my natural fatherly instinct to care for, protect and raise my son. There is nothing more important in my life. Admittedly, such dire circumstances shouldn't be required for a parent to make a firm commitment to his children, but the memories of that five-year-old boy helped me endure the many years of struggling it took to get custody of my son. I could not be deterred whereas others may have been.

In the years that followed, my mom was a giant among women. Again, she worked three jobs to provide for us, but always made time for my bother and I. Despite being dealt a tough hand, she was a stoic example of parental commitment, pride and an unflappable work ethic. She was our rock. I can remember being called out on an infield fly rule during a little-league game and she went bananas. How dare that umpire call me out when the ball hit the ground! I pleaded with her to sit down and let the game go on, but she just didn't understand that particular rule of the game. I could have wasted a lot of time as a kid being embarrassed by such things, but instead I cherished her love and dedication to Bobby and I. We were not wanting for strength and support.

During the next few years, my main father figure was my Uncle Doug on my mom's side of the family. He was kind, but stern, and not afraid to give me a walloping when I needed it, which was more often than not. I can remember what an absolutely fantastic master of the BBQ he was and we cherished our frequent visits to his house. We lived in trailers most of my childhood, but in his house I found my first taste of the American Dream. It was a modest home by standards back then, but it was spacious and well kept with nice furniture and a clean floor. They also had a pool where my brother and I would swim every weekend with our cousins. Those were good times, and when we were with them, I felt the strong sense of a complete family. Through that experience, I developed an ideal vision for the family I would have one day and the home in which we would live and grow together. I knew it would take hard work and dedication to get there. One doesn't leave behind the trailer lifestyle by dreaming about it. No, my American Dream would only be realized if I went after it with every ounce of determination I had within me.

My real dad, Frank Wurzelbacher, came into my live when I was nine years old. His meeting my mom is the sort of thing about which love stories are written. He first met her during a chance encounter at one of her jobs where she worked as a waitress. Her luck with men by that stage of her life left much to be desired, so she really didn't give him the time of day. Frank was a real gentleman and didn't pursue her beyond her interest, though he was definitely interested.

Two weeks later, Frank came into the local Salvation Army store, doing some bargain shopping when he pleasantly discovered my mom working behind the counter. Turns out, this was another of her three jobs. Feeling a little more ambitious he asked her out on a date. This time she agreed, perhaps feeling there was something more than coincidence at work. They courted for a month, going out frequently on dates and speaking over the phone almost constantly. Then it came time for my mom to introduce this stranger to her two boys. I'm sure she was nervous about it, but their love was budding fast and she had to know if he was going to be the kind of father we needed.

The first time I met Frank Wurzelbacher, an Air Force Staff Sergeant, it was Thanksgiving Day. As he walked in through our front door, I remember being impressed with his lean, clean-cut military-grade presence, yet he looked more like a cowboy just off the ranch in his flannel shirt, blue jeans and square-toed, brown boots. I felt I should have been suspicious about his intentions towards my mother. After all, what nine-year-old boy wouldn't be, considering all we had been through? Instead, I found myself immediately gravitating towards his upbeat and personable demeanor. He was very polite to my brother and I. He shook our hands and immediately engaged us in boy-talk. He seemed to take a genuine interest in who we were, our likes and dislikes, and what we did for fun. He talked to us about his job and how he could take us out on the flight line to watch Fighter Jets take off and land. That was COOL, but what I noticed right off the bat, was how he gave my mom the utmost respect. He treated her like a lady, and I liked that a lot.

As my mom prepared the feast, Frank took Bobby and I out to the woods to play. Somehow he knew exactly how to fit in. He didn't try to overcrowd us, but let us run around and be boys, joining in wherever it was comfortable. He was strong. He could lift both of us up off the ground, which impressed me, because I was a big kid for my age. He also took time to share with us some knowledge he had about the nature surrounding us. He pointed out the types of trees, the animal tracks on the ground and the bugs beneath the leaves. It was a prelude of his natural ability to instruct.

When we went to climb trees, he joined us. If we asked him a question, he answered it. I just couldn't shake this feeling that there was something really special about this guy. I had a deep and undeniable desire to have a positive male influence in my life. A man in the house, whom you can trust, brings with him a sense of security and stability. Don't misunderstand me, my mom was great, but no matter how wonderful she was, she couldn't be a dad. I needed a dad. I wanted one in the worst way. This Thanksgiving, my brother and I were given a taste of what it was like to have a real father. There was a five-year-old hole in my heart that I secretly dared hope this man might just be able to fill.

In all, it was a very special day. Somehow our home felt complete, like the sense I would feel at Uncle Doug's house. Over turkey dinner, Frank told us about his childhood, the kinds of things he liked to do as a boy, and then asked if we enjoyed the same. He wasn't playing a part. He really wanted to get to know us. When we sat down to watch football, he didn't just watch the game and hush the kids when we made noise, he taught us the game. When the time came for him to leave that evening, I felt that part of our home went with him. He was that great.

Not long after that first test, my mom decided to give Frank a tougher assignment—babysitting! Mom left Frank to watch us boys, as she had to go off to work. He wasn't the least bit intimidated, and I respected that. Nonetheless, being a nine-year-old, I had to put him to the test. After all, wasn't that what mom wanted? As we sat in the family room watching television, I got up and went to the kitchen, opened the freezer and pulled out a tub of ice cream. After fetching a spoon I came back, plopped down and proceeded to dig into this giant-sized tub of ice cream all by myself.

"Don't you need a bowl?" he asked me.

"Nope, this is how I always eat my ice cream."

"Hmmm," he grunted thoughtfully. He always was a patient and thoughtful man. Fortunately for me, he knew that the time to assert his authority over me had not yet come. I wasn't his son and he wasn't in his house. Again, it just goes to show his measure of respect for my mom. Rather than overstep his bounds, he ignored my antics and continued to treat my mom like a lady.

On Christmas Eve my mom received a call from the man who had abandoned us. He wanted to explain to my brother and I that he had a new life and that we weren't likely to see him again. By then, my mom was engaged to Frank, and I knew he was going to be the father I had always wanted. I replied to the stranger on the phone, "Mom's getting married and I'm gonna have a new dad, and he won't hit us. So, I don't want you to come back." That was the last I ever heard from him, and I have been forever grateful.

After just a three-month courtship, Frank married my mom and did indeed become my new dad. He has since been the only true father I have ever known, and it wasn't all playtime in the woods, either. I can remember when they got back from their honeymoon, which was just a motel getaway an hour or so down the highway. That night my mom and new dad took my brother and I to the movies to see *Snow White and the Seven Dwarfs*. I acted like a complete brat. I complained all night and sat through the entire movie with an ugly scowl on my face. It wasn't that I didn't like the movie, though that was my excuse. In reality, I was asserting my independence. I can't remember why I had felt a need to do so, but suffice it to say, my days of eating tubs of ice cream without a bowl were over. My dad had rules and consequences for those foolish enough to break them.

When we got home, he took me to my room and turned me to face him. Looking me sternly in the eyes, but without anger or rage, he said, "You are going to be disciplined for your behavior tonight. You did your best to ruin everyone else's time, and that was wrong. Do you understand?" I simply nodded and was promptly turned around and received three smacks from his belt. I wanted to laugh. I had suffered a great deal worse, but then I saw the look on his face. He wasn't drunk or in a fit of rage. His expression was a combination of sternness and disappointment. It cut deep, but I tried not to show it. Who was he to look at me this way? I had been the man of the house for the last five years. Didn't he know? I wanted a father, but I didn't know the first clue about what a father really was.

Growing up the way I had and learning some harsh lessons of life early on, I was about as ornery a kid as they come. I liked doing things my way and I didn't much care to respect anything. It surely wasn't in my nature to give any adult my automatic respect. How could I? I had seen firsthand how bad adults could be. In fact, I have taught my son today that respect has to be earned, regardless of age. It's dangerous to give it away for free. Now, that does not mean he can act like a complete jerk. Everyone deserves basic civility and common decency. However, in my view, if you teach your children to automatically accredit respect to an individual merely because he or she is an adult, you are opening them up to danger.

Anyhow, thank God my dad was up to the task with me. I kid you not; I felt the snap of his belt every day for that entire first year. I was about the worst combination of stubborn and dense as one can get. Nonetheless, my dad never faltered and never had a moment of inconsistency. He always explained to me what I had done wrong and what was expected of me. He never struck me in anger and never caused me any physical harm. His punishment was measured and just, and though I somehow couldn't get out of my misbehaving rut, I did appreciate that he was right and I was wrong.

I remember one particular occasion in the midst of that initial three hundred and sixty-four day attitude adjustment merry-go-round, when my dad sat me down and tried to reason with me. "Look Joe," he said, "it's about time you change this bad behavior. God hates liars, cheaters and thieves. Are you going to be one of them or are you going to set yourself straight and start respecting yourself and those around you?"

All of ten years old, I decided to break it to him. "Look dad, it's too late. I'm set in my ways."

That wasn't the answer my dad was looking for and thus the hard lessons continued. It wasn't that I didn't respect him, because I did more than any other man I knew. He had earned that right when I first saw how well he treated my mom. He further built upon it by always making my brother and I a priority in his life and by being consistent. Yes, the discipline of his belt was an important part of that consistency.

About a year into our father-son relationship, I asked my dad if I could use the eight-inch hunting knife my grandfather had willed to me to carve a four-inch stick. He said no. I asked him again and again, but he wouldn't budge. I wonder why he didn't think that was such a good idea? Despite my youthful ambition, when your dad tells you no, it means no.

Against his wishes and my better judgment, assuming I had any at that point in my life, I went and found a pair of scissors in my mom's utility cabinet. I figured they weren't as good as a knife, but they would do the job just fine. So, next thing you know, I'm out in the back carving up a stick with my mom's only pair of scissors. I wasn't long into the project when they suddenly broke in two. You know that dread you used to feel as a kid when you're doing something you know you're not supposed to and old Murphy comes to visit? Well, that was me.

I snuck into the house and put the broken scissors back in my mom's cabinet, expecting she wouldn't find them for days or perhaps weeks. By then, this stick-carving thing would be long forgotten and I could just play stupid. No sooner had I turned my back on my ill deed than this terrible feeling of guilt sank in my gut. I went back outside to play and tried to put it out of my head, but I couldn't shake that feeling. It was awful.

Finally, I just couldn't take it anymore. I went back inside, got the broken scissors and took them to my dad. Without hesitation, I fessed up about what I had done. I fully expected that he would greet me once again with the snap of his belt and another solemn lecture. I was wrong. Instead of the anticipated disappointment, my dad's eyes showed the admiration he felt for the quality I had at last discovered within myself. This was, by all reckoning the first time I had ever turned myself in. Another way of looking at it was that this was the first time I had learned the meaning of responsibility. I had always enjoyed my mom's love and affection, but now I had earned the respect of this man before me, a man whom I admired above all.

From that point on, I was a different kid. Sure, I still made mistakes and I had many more lessons to learn, but I really did my absolute best to not lie anymore. This was just one example of what an incredible difference my dad made in our family.

After my dad came into our lives, he became the rock upon which we all could lean. My mom was able to cut back to just one job and begin to enjoy her children more. Through my dad, my brother and I learned to become men, and we learned the joys of having a father. He made us a priority. Whether playing a game of pickle with Bobby and I in the yard, or having a catch with the football, or making sure we applied ourselves with our schooling, he never turned us down for the time we needed with him. He was tough too, which made you want to try harder. Where it came to our education, he never gave us the simple answer. Instead he would make you go and look things up. Sometimes punishment was meted out in the form of having to read five pages of the dictionary. He also made us read the newspaper and news magazines. He was, and remains a firm believer in the truth that knowledge is power. It is from him that I learned the phrase, *"Get educated, get informed."* Those were really my dad's words, not mine.

My dad also wouldn't suffer my brother and I to do anything without a solid plan. For something as mundane as building a birdhouse, he would say, "Where are your plans? You aren't going to build a decent house for those birds if you don't have a plan." He wasn't a great builder, himself, but his astute power of logic and dedication allowed him to perfect almost any trade or individual task he put his mind to. That is how I learned to believe in my own ability to do things I had never done, whether I knew where to start. Through my dad I learned that in order to succeed, one must follow a logical course to achieve any goal and that seldom, if ever, are there shortcuts.

Once more, it's all about hard lessons. I can remember watching Bengals games with my dad on Sundays, but sometimes losing interest and having an urge to go and do something else. That's typical and normal for kids, right? Well, I would always stay with him and remain engaged. Why? Because it always felt good to be near him, to share his time and be wanted in return. Were it not for all the hardships we had endured before my dad came along, I'm not sure any of us would have appreciated just how great a gift God had given us. Neither do I believe we would have realized how much we needed him on so many levels. I shudder to think how many bad things would have happened in my life. Today, I understand that beside the highways of success and happiness are the littered re-mains of those tragic souls who never discovered the meaning of self-respect or a sense of personal responsibility. I didn't teach myself that lesson, my dad did, and he wasn't afraid of how hard it was going to be to instill such things in me.

I could go on and on about the hard lessons I learned during my youth, or as a young adult or what I learned yesterday, but you have your own life's lessons to reflect upon. My basic point is that everyone feels good after a hard day's work. Accomplishment gives one a greater sense of importance and fulfillment than if you never strive to achieve anything. It feels especially good to do physical labor, to sweat and to see your labors materialize before you. Some of the things I enjoy more than anything else are digging holes and chopping wood. Yes, it's hard work, but it's honest. You can't cheat and there are no shortcuts. This is a lesson of life, which may be why one of our great presidents, Theodore Roosevelt, once stated that, *"Far and away the best prize that life offers is the chance to work hard at work worth doing."*

5

Serving My Country

There are few things I believe in more than duty and service. When I spoke about my *civic duty* during the many interviews I gave to media all across this country and throughout the world, it was not a punch line nor was it something merely convenient to say. One of the great travesties in this country is our selfishness as a people. The further we get from conflict against the evils of the world, the greater this sentiment pervades our national consciousness. It begins with our youth and spreads like a rash from generation to generation. Does this mean I'm one of those types who seek conflict? No, not at all, but the fact of the matter is that until the end of time, there will always be evil forces at work, whose mission will be to strip away the freedoms of others and to enslave their fellow man. Ask yourself during which period in history this wasn't the case. Everlasting peace has never been, and until it comes we must remain vigilant and sworn to serve and protect our treasures, our freedoms and the future of our children. If you have never made service to your country a priority in your life, I recommend you rethink what it means and consider joining the military, or at least outwardly supporting our men and women in uniform in whatever capacity you can.

I come from a long history of family members who have given their service and their blood to preserve our American Dream. Wurzelbachers have defended our country in every conflict since the Revolutionary War. Let me make something clear, however, that this is not a bragging right. It is a solemn duty.

My grandfather was an infantry soldier during World War II. He fought at the Battle of Guadalcanal, which history would come to regard as the turning point of that war. It was the first significant victory for the Allied Forces over Japan in the Pacific theater. Now ask yourself, how would we have achieved this victory and thus taken a great step towards securing our freedoms here at home, were it not for the bravery and dedication of American soldiers like my grandfather? The answer is simple. We would have failed and would have become slaves to the Japanese on a biblical scale. Just read a little about the horrors that Imperial Japan reaped upon China.

Something else about my grandfather that made a distinct impression on me, and my father before me, was that he never spoke about the war. I can remember seeing his worn and faded Marine tattoo on his arm and asking if he fought in the war. He never said a word about it. He would just look at me with a penetrating stare, probably circulating through his mind the great many reasons why I had no business knowing, nor could I understand. Even a pestering kid who has always had a habit of asking direct questions couldn't get it out of him. Today, I respect him for that. War stories are for those who fought and bled together on the battlefield. The results of their sacrifices are for the rest of us.

Years later when my grandfather passed away, we learned from his sister that he had spent time as a Japanese POW. In fact, my great-aunt had newspaper clippings from his period of service, heralding his heroism and sacrifice. Whatever happened to him in the war had changed him forever. As a kid, he used to love rice pudding. Coming back from the war, he never ate a grain of rice again in his life, nor would he suffer anyone to eat it in his presence.

Makes you wonder what happened, doesn't it? There may be no one alive today who knows the answer to that question anymore. I suppose that's the proper order of things. All we need to know it that we can walk outside our homes today, enjoy the sunshine, play ball in the yard and challenge a politician who may come walking down our street without any fear of reprisal. At least, that's how it is supposed to be.

Growing up in a family where virtually every man either was or had been in the service, including my Air Force father, I had no question about what I would do when my opportunity came to serve. In order to prepare for it, I joined the Army JROTC in high school. The Junior Reserve Officers Training Corps, as it is lesser known, is a program sponsored by our various military branches intended to make better citizens of our youth, through discipline and commitment to a code of character and service to our country. Now what can be wrong with that? Some would claim this program is all about war mongering, which is absolutely nuts!

Case in point; in November 2006 the San Francisco School Board voted to eliminate the JROTC from its schools. Why? It seems the wise old school board members realized that this program was a recruitment tool for the military. No way, really? They also didn't like that if our young men and women joined the military, they might kill or be killed in a conflict, which our president may determine we as a country needed to engage. Instead, they wanted to teach peace not war. Sounds a bit like *make love not war* doesn't it. Whatever happened to people making their own choices? Oh, I see, our high-school kids are just too stupid to know what's best for them. That, too, sounds like another familiar theme in politics.

So let me get this straight, we shouldn't be recruiting from our young men and women to serve in the military, because that might mean they have to go to war? Well, who in the world is going to fight our conflicts then, France? You have got to be kidding me! What is the prerequisite for being on the San Francisco School Board anyhow, ten years of Socialist indoctrination at Berkeley? I readily recognize that some of these people and those that support them are just plain stupid. Sorry, but there is no other word for it—actually there are plenty, but I want to keep this book clean. Nonetheless, those of you who still have, at the least, greater brain function than a gerbil must realize that there is a conspiracy in this country to weaken us to the point of extinction. Yes, I realize I said earlier I'm not a *Big Conspiracy* theorist, but on this account I can't think of a better explanation. It's not about paranoia. I'm coming to this conclusion based upon logic and reason. Listen, if you think that war is evil, I agree with you. If you think that those who make war are evil, I'm inclined to agree with you there too. If you think that all those who engage in war are evil or that war can always be avoided, I couldn't disagree with you more. The day America abandons our commitment to military strength and future defense development will be the day we put the wheels in motion for our enemies to one day invade and carry away our children for slaves. Indeed, we will look upon that day with our heads bowed low and our Flag in ashes and say, *that was the turning point.*

Where was I? Oh yes, I belonged to the JROTC in my high school, and to my knowledge they haven't outlawed it there yet. It was a program that helped me model myself after the kinds of examples I had seen in my father, my uncles and the line of our generations back to the founding of this country. In addition to my peaceful studies, I learned about discipline, loyalty and a military code of ethics. We learned how to read topographical maps, basic marksmanship, military procedures, and became certified in four basic life saving techniques, such as CPR. We also had to endure a physically challenging two-week boot camp. Does that sound scary?

The most rewarding aspect of my time with the JROTC was leading the Drill Team, and we were one of the best units in the country. Drilling is where you perform highly disciplined marching procedures with rifles. Our outfit was so good we traveled all throughout the country winning one competition after another. It was all about *snap and pop.* We were tight. We were disciplined. We were just plain good and proud of it.

Shortly after high school, I was faced with the decision about which branch of the military in which to enlist. No, it wasn't a question of if, just under which branch. I suppose that proves the San Franciscans right, doesn't it. God forbid I should want to serve my country! My girlfriend at the time, who later became my wife, helped me make this important decision. Originally, I really wanted to be a Marine, Force Recon. Ultimately, however, I decided to follow in my father's footsteps and went with the Air Force. My intent was to become a Crew Chief, performing service and maintenance on F-16 Fighter Jets. It was said to be a high-stakes, stress-filled job due to the critical importance of doing one's work well. One foul-up and you could cost the American taxpayer a hundred million-dollar plane, or worse you might get a pilot killed.

During orientation for boot camp, a classroom of new recruits, including myself, were put to several questions to determine our motivations for joining the military. One by one the questions were put forth regarding one military perk or another, and yet I never raised my hand. One question for which everyone else raised their hand was the GI Bill.

Finally, the Drill Sergeant came over to me and asked in the usual polite, soft-spoken and congenial manner of all Drill Sergeants, "Private, BLEEPITY, BLEEP-BLEEP! If you didn't join up for the GI Bill, then what the BLEEP did you join for!"

"Duty to serve my country, Drill Sergeant!"

He didn't question me for a second, because those guys know how to sniff out B.S. better than I do. I'm not saying the GI Bill or any other benefit the military gives to our service men and women is bad by any stretch. In fact, I believe they deserve more. Yet, I have always believed that to serve a country as great as the United States of America is a profound and sacred honor. My attitude is, as it was then, that *service* is not supposed to be about reward. Sure, a great many rewards in many forms usually result from a commitment to service, but that's not why you are supposed to do it. What meaning does service have if a measure is only given in anticipation of the measure that will be received in return?

Boot camp wasn't as much of a challenge as it would have been, were it not for my JROTC experience. When I graduated, I went to sign up for tech-school for my new F-16 mechanic trade, but you already know the rest of that story. If I wanted to stay in the Air Force, I needed to pick something else, so Plumber it was!

I married my girlfriend right after plumber tech school, before I was given my first assignment. Where? *The Call of the Wild*, remember? Doug, my best friend at the time and still is, went to plumbing tech school with me and was also assigned to Alaska. I guess I was less than sane by normal standards, but I could hardly contain my excitement. My wife was leery about it from the beginning. It was, after all, about three thousand miles away from any family and about the farthest place away from the world either of us had known. Still, we had each other and that was good enough for high-school sweethearts in love, as we embarked on our first journey of life together. Yes, I can hear Sonny and Cher singing in the background too.

We initially flew into Fairbanks, Alaska en route to Eielson Air Force Base. From the plane, I got a sneak preview of the grandeur that awaited. The snowcapped mountains in the distance were just magnificent, the likes of which I had never seen before nor have I since. They dwarfed the lush landscape, snaked by hundreds of waterways, below. I almost forgot I was a military man. I think I could have disappeared into that wilderness and have never come back. Ultimately, it proved to be everything I could have hoped for and more.

Nevertheless, here is where reality sets in. After initially checking in with the Senior Master Sergeant and moving into temporary quarters on base, our first order of business wasn't plumbing for the United States Air Force. No, it wasn't to go sightseeing either. The single greatest challenge from day one in the military remained a challenge until my last day in the service—Housing! Before I go on, let me make it clear that I believed, and still believe, that service is about honor first and everything else second. However, when you consider all the waste in government spending year after year, what excuse is there for not providing ample housing for our military men and women? In my humble opinion . . . never mind, it's just plain B.S.!

If you have never served in the military, then you probably never thought of housing being a problem, yet it is widely felt by nearly all enlisted families. We fell into the enlisted category, and thus immediately applied for two things: First, we got ourselves on the *on-base housing* waiting list—a long waiting list. Second, we went in search of an apartment nearby and applied for BAQ, which is Basic Allowance for Quarters. Here's the problem; BAQ almost never covers the entire cost of off-base housing. We are not talking about a situation where us military-folk are seeking luxury living either. If you are, it's not remotely and option, so why waste time dreaming. Considering the miserable pay one gets in the military, a forty-dollar a month BAQ deficit for an apartment can be huge, and is often insurmountable. I suppose the logic on Capitol Hill is that when you serve in the military everything is paid for, so why would you need much pay? Well, ask any military family and they'll give you a long laundry list of bills and necessities that are not covered by Uncle Sam. The simple point is that we can do better. No one should expect to get rich in the military serving our country. For that matter, no one should expect to reap much of any material reward. However, we should make sure that our service men and women have little to worry about so they can apply all their focus to the important jobs they do while securing our freedoms.

We spent our first year in a town called the North Pole. Awesome right? You get to live near Santa's elves and you're first every year on Santa's gift drop. In reality, I spent that first year fixing urinals, toilets, sinks, flushometers, wells, and boilers. I repiped or setup new waterlines, drain lines, and established backflow devices to keep potable water safe. Whether a dirty job, not so dirty job or only slightly dirty job I had a hand in it all at some point. I learned early on that the extreme climate conditions up there require extra precautions, reinforcement measures and sometimes a sense of humor.

Just to give you an example of what the climate is like, three feet of snow dropped the day after we landed in Fairbanks. We wouldn't see green or anything remotely warm for another eight months. Oh yeah it was cold, the likes of which I have never experienced anywhere else. Layered clothing was IN, and I mean things like Mukluks, extra-thick long underwear, super-thick mittens and Bunny Boots. Temperatures up there can drop to as low as sixty below. Yeah, it was cold all right—or did I mention that already?

One day, Doug and I got called out to one of the flight line buildings to respond to a complete blowout of the structure's entire water piping system. When we arrived and walked inside, it was like one of those submarine movies where the sub gets bombarded by depth charges and leaks burst out all over the place. Come to find out, the power in the building had gone out and with it the heaters. Without heat, the building quickly turned into a giant ice-cube and so the pipes burst. We spent about twenty minutes searching the place for the main shutoff valve, but couldn't find it. Finally, we realized that it was outside. Problem was, we were soaking wet now, and although it was daylight, we are talking about Alaska. It was thirty below outside! Regardless, we were young and dealing with an emergency, so we dashed outside and ran around the building until we got to the shutoff valve and cut the water flow.

Shivering uncontrollably, we trotted back around the building to get back inside and inspect the damage. We had hardly gone ten feet when Doug suddenly pointed at me and said, "Dude, look at your jacket!"

I looked down and saw that my jacket had literally frozen and cracked in several places, almost like I was wearing papier mache. Doug began to laugh, but then I pointed out his jacket had cracked open in several places as well. We kind of looked at each other with disbelief, and then naturally we proceeded to test more areas of each other's jackets to see how much of it would break. When we had exhausted the ice buildup, did we return to our job or go home for the day? Of course not, we went back in the building got wet again and came back outside to see if our jackets would crack open some more, which they did. Yep, that's just one example of the kind of fun you can have while plumbing in the subzero temperatures of Alaska.

Despite the cold, the wilderness of Alaska is just breathtaking. I can't say enough about it. No picture can do it justice and certainly no description of mine. When I wasn't plumbing, I was hiking, fishing and occasionally hunting. You have to see it to understand the absolute majesty of that land. It is nothing less than the last and ultimate frontier of America. You feel smothered by nature in all its glory, and it feels like heaven. At night, the aurora borealis wave in colossal brilliant ribbons of green, blue, purple and pink. Beyond its mesmerizing light are stars so large and bright you feel you can reach right out and pluck them from the sky. Folks, it is nothing short of spectacular. Still, don't go up there with any misgivings about a luxury vacation of bliss and hot cocoa. Life up there is tough as it gets and it can be deadly if you make the mistake of failing to respect the awesome power of the elements and the wildlife.

I'll never forget the second time I met a bear, and yes it happened more than once. The first time I ran into a bear, I was just a kid wandering the woods back in Louisiana. Walking along off the beaten path, I darn near tripped over him. Whoa! There he was, a black bear standing on all fours right in front of me. Fortunately, he didn't pay me much mind, but instead grumbled a little and walked off. Black bears can be dangerous, although they do not nearly measure up to the physical specimen of the American Grizzly.

During my second year in Alaska I went out for a hike late one morning to take in the scenery and relieve some of the stresses of life. It is easy to lose yourself in the peacefulness of nature out there, despite the fact that many dangers are lurking. I was having such a moment when I came around a bend and froze with a shock. I founded myself treacherously standing within five feet of a large and ferocious-looking grizzly! It was like staring at a truck, but alive with sharp teeth, long razor-like claws and a killer instinct. He had a full winter coat on and an extra helping of blubber for the upcoming hibernation season, during which time these bears get to be twice their normal size. But don't be fooled, he could still run down an Olympic sprinter, which I was not. He rose up on his hind legs to a height of almost six and a half feet tall! I pretty well figured bye-bye Joe. My rifle was slung across my back and my sidearm was holstered on my hip. Had he charged me, I would have been dead before I had gotten a chance to make any move for a weapon, let alone turn and run. I kept telling myself over and over again, *Don't breathe too fast, don't move, stand still and don't be afraid.* Almost any animal, but particularly predators can sense fear. The slightest motion or expression of intimidation on my part could easily encourage this great beast to attack.

Even as I contemplated my impending doom, thinking about my wife and all I had to live for, I could not get past the sheer awesomeness of this animal before me. His black menacing eyes were deep and penetrating. I got the feeling he was figuring me out, just as I was analyzing him. We humans believe we are so great, and we are in many ways. Yet, to face an intelligent creature like a bear, with superior power, speed, agility and the ability to survive the harshest elements with no skill to build or craft, is just humbling beyond compare. At that moment, I can tell you that I respected that bear a great deal more than most people I had ever met.

It felt like we stood there for a lifetime, but it was only a couple of minutes. After looking me over a bit and sniffing the air as though he wanted to determine whether I might be a good meal, he finally dropped to all fours again. I was not threatening to him in the least. In fact, he gave me a derisive grunt, as if to say *you stink* or *you are not worth my time*, and ambled off into the woods in a lackadaisical manner that belied his deadly speed. I continued to hold my ground, wondering if he were going to pop out of another part of the woods and yet attack me. However, I was mostly stupefied by the encounter. Scared as I was, it was an absolutely incredible experience and I was grateful for it. God bless Alaska!

After our second year up there, we finally saw our turn for on-base housing come around. That was good, because living off base with little means to sustain us was tough. We never had more than just enough to put food on the table and buy layered clothing. The closest thing we had to a piece of furniture was a sofa worn down to the wood that someone else had thrown out. It wasn't the most comfortable thing to sit on, but with a few blankets and makeshift cushions, it did the job. In the military, that's about all you can afford.

Above all, the Alaskan experience, about which I had dreamt so long throughout my youth, was marred by a mysterious illness that took wife by storm on only the third day of our arrival. She had constant abdominal pains and fatigue. She slept all through the night and most of each day. Because of the constant pain and other symptoms, she also wasn't the most fun to be around. That really put a strain on a young marriage, but I was committed to stand by her *in sickness* if not *in health.* I had, after all, taken that oath for my wife under God.

After months and months of visits with doctors and countless tests, she was finally diagnosed with endometriosis, a condition that would persist the entire time we lived in Alaska. We didn't get to enjoy each other or nearly enough of the rare and special place in which we were so blessed to live for a time. I guess that's life. Make all the fine plans you like, but something unexpected will always come your way.

Another great challenge for us was that we had been trying for a child ever since we had arrived, but it just wasn't panning out for whatever reason. Unlike her illness, no doctor or man-made test could tell us what the problem was. After two years of no luck, we figured we just weren't going to be the kind of family we each had hoped for. I was supremely disappointed, because my vision of a family and the American Dream had been so deeply etched into my mind. But what are you going to do? You have to play the cards God deals you, and they aren't always the ones you like. So, we went out and bought a dog and resolved ourselves to raising puppies instead of children. Two weeks later, she was pregnant!

We were naturally thrilled, but now that we had a child coming we also had a great dilemma with finances, or the lack thereof, as was our case. This is yet another area of the military that just bites. Because you do not get a pay raise for growing your family beyond a spouse, having children means that both parents must work. There is no other option. If, in our case, my wife did not get a job, we could not afford to buy formula, baby clothes or diapers, let alone a crib or a home with an extra room in which to place it. I suppose the military didn't ask me to join to procreate, so why should they have to pay for it. I guess I can think of a few good reasons, one of which would be that I believe our military families are uniquely suited for raising the next generation of American patriots. However, when both parents are working instead of raising their children, just who is instilling those patriotic values?

Like I said, I love the military. I believe in the honor of serving my country with every fiber of my being. Nonetheless, I believe that we as a country can do better by our service men and women. We certainly provide for many families who offer little to nothing in return. In an institution that may at any time call its volunteers into war and potentially make orphans of the children they bring into this world, one would think it a small matter to ensure they have, at the least, proper food, clothing and housing.

The one thing we could do that wasn't going to cost anything was pick names, which was easy. If it were a boy he would be named Joey, after me. If it were a girl, well, what do you think about the name Joey? I guess God sent us a boy so that we wouldn't have to worry about that.

If naming our child wasn't a concern, my wife's condition and its bearing on our growing child inside her was. Aside from the physical challenges, talk to any woman of normal sound health and she'll tell you that being pregnant not only drains your energy and takes a significant physical toll, but it constantly bombards your emotions. Worse yet, Joey kept trying to come early. This is a traumatic experience for any family that has lived it, but when you add in the heartache we had in believing we weren't capable of conception, it hurts all the more. Those were an especially difficult and stressful eight months for me, and you can imagine they weren't much fun for my wife either.

Oh, did I say eight months? One would have thought Joey had an urgent appointment with destiny, because he would not be denied his entry into United States citizenship! That day was the greatest and most stressful of my life, without a doubt. We had left the hospital just hours earlier after having been there all night under a labor false alarm. The doctors eventually figured it wasn't time just yet, which was a reasoned error in judgment, because we had been going into and out of labor for months. What was one month more? Well, too long where Joey was concerned.

When we finally got home it was around 8am. I had been up since rising for work the prior day at 5am, so I was thoroughly beat and went straight to sleep. My wife had initially joined me, but I later discovered she had gotten out of bed to walk off some labor pains.

Perhaps only an hour into sleep, I was gently awakened by a tugging on my arm. Bleary-eyed I look up into her pained face as she said, "My water broke!"

"What?" I wasn't really awake.

"My water broke," she repeated in a strained voice. She had been experiencing the dreaded *back labor* for more than twelve hours now.

Dosing off, I said, "Don't worry about it. Remember that lady next door? Her water broke and she didn't have her baby for another week." With that, I fell asleep again. I know that sounds cruel, but you have to understand that we had been going through labor for almost the entire eight months of pregnancy. We hadn't experienced actual childbirth before and so neither of us really had any idea what to expect. For all we knew, Joey had another month to go.

After sleeping another hour or so, I heard the bloodcurdling scream from downstairs, "I'm having a baby!"

I shot up out of bed and ran downstairs. I didn't know where I was or what was happening at first, but my wife clearly had something going on!

I arrived at a scene I will never forget. She was laying half-naked on the living-room floor and desperately trying not to push. I had never seen her is such pain. I remember looking to see if Joey had come, but he wasn't showing yet. Without hesitation I ran for the phone and then returned to catch the baby if he came before help arrived. With one hand dialing 911 and the other held in a catching position, I got a dispatcher on the line, told the woman the situation, gave her my address and then hung up as I began to see Joey crown!

My wife was doing everything she could to not push, but her body, and Joey, had other ideas. As Joey's head started to come out and his eyes and nose became exposed, I remember having this rush of exhilaration and pure joy like nothing else I have ever experienced in my life. It was terribly frightening and completely awe-inspiring at the same time. I was witnessing life, but more than that, I was experiencing God's miracle of life.

Just in the nick of time, my door burst open and in stormed a nurse, a doctor and a group of firemen, many of whom I knew. It was an awkward situation, having your wife fully exposed to the general public, but I guess that's childbirth. There's no time for modesty and pleasantries. Quickly, the doctor moved into catching position and I moved over to the side. My wife finally allowed herself a real push and out Joey sprang. Yeah, a boy! No, we didn't ruin the traditional surprise.

The doctor and nurse cleaned Joey up a bit, sucking out his airways, and then the doctor offered me the honor of cutting the umbilical cord, which I gladly accepted. After that, the doctor put Joey on his mother's bosom and wrapped them both in a warm blanket for a nice peaceful ride in the ambulance to the hospital.

I made a couple of quick phone calls to family to announce our new arrival, then jumped in my car and raced to the hospital myself. When I arrived, the nurses were working Joey over with the normal bathing, measuring, examining and testing they do with newborns. Joey didn't care for it one bit, and seeing my tiny little boy in such distress really bothered me. I knew these things had to be done, but I had an overwhelming urge to protect him. When finally I got to hold him, I remember having this resolute sense that I was never going to let him go. He was so tiny and fragile to me. I couldn't stop looking at his miniature hands and feet. This was my son. I HAD A SON! There are no words in the English language that can justifiably describe those early moments with my son. I knew my bond with this boy was going to be special. I could feel it all the way through me and into my soul. This was my son, and I was going to do right by him, no matter what it took.

Let me sum up this chapter by reasserting that the most important thing we can do as a country to preserve our freedoms is to support the military. Every time I hear a politician complain about how much this country spends on defense, I say double it. Get our men and women of the armed services everything they need and then some. Did you know that the standard protocol for military families having children is to apply for WIC? That's Welfare for crying out loud! We are making our greatest citizens go on WELFARE! Surely, we can do better for them than that.

Perhaps if we made life in the military a little less pride swallowing where basic living needs are concerned we wouldn't have a recruitment problem. In fact, I'm a proponent of a mandatory term of service for every citizen, such as they do in Israel. Why? Well, aside from the great citizens the military molds and the values they instill, let me tell you why they do it in Israel. They have to. It's really that simple, because reality over there is that they are surrounded by their enemies. They are always under threat of invasion. In fact, legions of their enemies would invade them tomorrow if they weren't afraid of getting their butts kicked. The one thing that Israel's enemy-neighbors understand is that every man, woman and young adult in that country knows how to fight. It's a simple fact of life that bullies don't pick on the kids in the neighborhood who are accustomed to fighting back.

Some of you may sympathize with the San Franciscan viewpoint that military service is a negative thing, or at least want to believe that militarization of a society leads to war. I beg to differ. I believe that training our young people to defend this country will only breed good, and less conflict. It will make our enemies think even harder before they jump into the ring with us. Also, in this country it is a fact of law that our elected officials hold the power with which to make and engage in war. Furthermore, history has shown that neither party in American politics has a monopoly on exercising that power. So, if we wind up in a war *We The People* don't want, don't we have only ourselves to blame for electing the officials that take us into that war? Instead of trying to subvert the military, why don't the San Francisco Board of Education and all their sympathizers focus on electing better politicians? Either they are too incompetent to be educating our youth, or they have ulterior motives. That, folks is something we all need to be very concerned about, because nothing spoke louder to me after the experience of my son's birth than my duty to protect and defend his future.

6

Pursuing The American Dream

When you think about the American Dream, what comes to mind? Do you see a large sprawling ranch in the countryside or do you see a sky-rise condo overlooking Central Park? Do you envision yourself riding over the hills on horseback or flying down the highway in something that has a 900 horsepower engine? Are the dreams of your childhood, or of your children today, present anywhere within that picture?

The older I get, the further my childhood dreams drift from consciousness. In fact, as an adult it's a challenge to remember the period in my life where dreams were remotely acceptable. When I was a kid, my dreams were pure and unfettered by the experiences older folks would suggest brings forth wisdom. While I agree that age and wisdom are somewhat tied together, I see too many examples of how life teaches pessimism and embittering complacency more than it does anything else. I often wonder whether it will be the aspirations of our youth or the jaded and selfish notions of the supposed older and wiser that will dictate the future of our country and our American Dream.

My first love as a kid was for animals. I took in every stray dog, bird and cat that crossed my path. I nursed them back to health, trained them in whatever capacity was at my disposal and would hence beg my mom and dad to let me keep them. It drove them nuts, but I think they appreciated my passion for it. I had initially aspired to become a veterinarian, but later abandoned the idea. Though I wasn't an awful student, straight A's were not a part of my report card. Without the kinds of grades necessary to get a scholarship, college was about as financially realistic an option as hopping a flight to the moon. Unfortunately, my desire to become a veterinarian would have to remain a dream.

When I reached the fifth grade, I found a new love in science, and specifically with Astronomy. I owe this inspiration to Mrs. Vercelloti. It began through her lessons about Greek mythology and its close relationship with star constellations like Orion, Cygnus and others. I then began to study more about our universe. I read every book I could find on the subject and became absolutely captivated by things like black holes, red dwarfs, quarks, quasars, supernovas and anything else there was to know about the great unknown of space. When I got to the sixth grade my parents managed to scrape enough of their hard-earned pennies together to get me a telescope. It was the single best gift I received throughout all my childhood. I spent countless nights out in remote fields with it, laying back and studying the stars without ever tiring. I would take friends with me, who thought it was cool at first, but would soon get bored. Not I. Long after they had gone home, I remained, marveling over the vast and infinite reaches of our universe.

My aspirations in life revolved around Astronomy up through my junior year in high school. Once again, however, I was daunted by the reality of choosing this as a profession in life. Aside from the necessary college education, which I clearly could not afford, everything I researched about it painted a humbling picture. I discovered that studying the final frontier was not a lucrative field of interest. In fact, most astronomers lived by grants, which only provided a humble living at best and often didn't last. Nonetheless, I probably would have stuck with it had my telescope not been stolen one night. I had gone out with a friend to set up my mobile observatory at one of my many ideal stargazing spots. After a few hours of awe and marvel, we loaded up the car to go, but it wouldn't start! We locked it up, deciding to head home on foot and return for the car the next day with help. Unfortunately, when we returned the next day, the car had been broken into. Among the many things taken was the greatest treasure of my childhood. Money to buy another one was hardly an option, and so another of my childhood dreams slipped through reality's grasp.

You already know my young adult story. I was an Air Force plumber, and avid outdoorsman and became a young father by the age of twenty-one. Despite every dream I had ever had, nothing could have prepared me for the sweeping life changes of fatherhood. If you are a parent, and you have never taken a moment to look back at all that defined your life prior to becoming a parent versus after, then take a moment now . . .

Wow! What a difference, right? If you're saying not really, then frankly you scare me. When Joey arrived, nothing was about me anymore. I quickly came to understand that my new life's purpose was he. It was my duty to instill in him the lessons of life and survival, and to equip him with the tools necessary to excel at whatever he set his mind to. He, my son, became my American Dream and everything else I had ever known fell to a distant second.

The great irony with having a focus on the dreams of your children is that most, if not all of your childhood dreams, quickly fall by the wayside. If you belong to the few whose dream directly contributed or is contributing to the dreams of your children, then you are truly blessed. I, on the other hand, belong to the much larger crowd who, in order to provide and care for the dreams of our children, must do things that are often the antithesis of what we wanted to do in life.

At the end of my third year in the Air Force in Alaska, I got the distinct sense that the challenges ahead were going to put both my faith and my belief in the American Dream to task. Although I wouldn't admit it at the time, my marriage to Joey's mom was failing. Despite all my efforts, I just couldn't find that magic bean that would grow a tree to a better place. Within a couple of years after leaving the military, our marriage was over. We became a part of a sadly typical American story, and my American Dream was shattered.

This was one of the most challenging and difficult periods in my life for so many reasons. In addition to the failure of my marriage, my father was struck by a sudden and almost deadly brain aneurysm. Overnight, the strength and mental greatness of my father had been reduced to the point where I didn't recognize him anymore. In many ways the care he gave me as a child was now needed from me to help him in his recovery.

Now a plumber by trade, I also had the problem of integrating back into civilian life working for large plumbing companies that seemed to care less about my livelihood than had the military. Whereas working for a private company brought forth the promise of a better income than I had yet seen, the hours and commitment that job required were just terrible. I was hardly home. I don't mind working long hard days, but consistency in the workday is key to balance with family. I worked twelve to sixteen-hour days, six and often seven days a week, and had to respond to jobs at all hours of the day and night. I had nothing resembling a consistent schedule around which I could plan my family time. I would have traded this for my time as an Air Force plumber in Alaska in a heartbeat, but it was too late to go back.

The most urgent matter before me was staying near my son, that I might remain a solid figure in his life. That priority took me on a path that led to Arizona, where Joey's mom had decided she wanted to live to be near her family. At first, I stuck with the plumbing trade, but I soon discovered that I didn't like the vision of my future with this particular job. All the tenured guys I worked with were beat down and filled with remorse over having missed their family life, now that their children had grown up. To hear them talk about it scared me to death. I could not and would not be that kind of father to Joey. He deserved better, especially with his mom and I being split up.

Just when I needed it the most, a better job opportunity did indeed come my way. That's America for ya. If you're willing to work hard and persevere, I have always found that the breaks do eventually come. It may sound strange to you, but I made a relatively seamless transition from plumbing to telecommunications. In a way, they both pertain to a network of pipelines, but that is where similarities end. The important thing about my new career is that by applying myself with dedication and a strong work ethic, I was able to excel in a field for which I had no prior knowledge. In fact, it took three short years for me to more than double the income I had earned as a plumber. Even better, I worked Monday through Friday, mostly nine to five and had all my weekends to give to Joey. Gotta love America!

The telecommunications job was good to me. I made good money, worked normal hours and had free time with my son. I was living the American Dream, right? Well, not quite. Fact is, a weekend dad was not enough for my son. He deserved better. In spite of that, his mother and I were trying to settle that issue in the courts. All the extra money I made during that period went into a giant vacuum of legal fees and child support. I didn't mind the latter one bit, but the legal fees one has to bear to battle out a custody dispute is just insane. Three years went by, feeling like three decades. I worked, I slept, I visited Joey on the weekends, and I worked some more. Really, there was nothing more in my life and dreams were a distant and vague memory.

Just when I felt I was stuck in an inescapable rut, I was sprung by fate. My great telecom employer decided to move my job overseas, along with many others. Count your blessings when you can, because what was I going to do now? I almost had a nervous breakdown. Without that job I couldn't make child support payments, couldn't pay attorneys and therefore would not be allowed to see Joey, and he was all that I was living for.

That night after my layoff, I prayed long and hard in search of deliverance. I was as lost as one can get, but in the midst of my prayers the answer came. Somehow, I knew that I needed to move back home to Toledo and that everything would be all right. I know it sounds weird. What about Joey, the custody battle, child support? I don't know how to explain it. I just had this distinct feeling deep within that told me to trust in my faith and that the answers to my troubles would come. It was like a voice in my soul that said, *Joe, you are going to move back to Ohio and all will be well.* This was one of the many times in my life where, without God, I would have been lost down a dark and lonely road, from which there may have been no return.

Over the next couple of days, I called home and began making my plans to move back. When the weekend came, I was greeted by a surprise visit from Joey's mom. It was welcomed, but unexpected. Furthermore, she wanted us to raise Joey back home in Toledo and was willing to move back as well to see that happen. I could hardly believe it. I had not told her yet what my plans were, and here my prayers had been answered in a most undeniable manner. I felt humbled by the blessing and realization that my dream to remain a fixture in my son's life had been granted.

After moving back to Toledo, I began to rebuild my life. I eventually regained my right to be a full-time father again, I had family near, friends with whom I could rekindle relationships and I could hopefully jumpstart my career. I worked a few odd jobs, when telecom came calling again—no pun intended. They realized I had done good work for them and they really wanted me back. The only problem was that I had to commute ninety miles to and from their nearest office. Nevertheless, it was an opportunity to reclaim my space on the corporate ladder and make some good money once more. At the time, I thought this was essential for my plans to make a real family life for Joey and I, which included buying a house. So I returned to the rut, and with a new role and long commute in hock, my days strangely began to resemble that time I spent as a corporate plumber. Days melded with nights and weekdays seeped over into weekends.

Not long into my reunion with telecom Joey came over to me and said, "Hey dad, how come whenever we're together, you're always busy working?"

My boy said it with the innocence only a child can deliver to his parent. I heard it loud and clear. He needed more of my time, and having keen childhood memories of my own, I knew that this simple question belied the desperation in his heart. Surely, I hadn't worked nine long and hard years just to have him sleeping in the same house as I. Somehow, my focus on creating a family life with Joey was having the exact opposite effect. Isn't life strange that way? We kill ourselves at a job day in and day out to provided for our children, when in fact, what our children need most is the thing God gave us from the beginning—our time.

What I quickly discovered that day, at the prompting of my son, is that *the job* was not the American Dream. No, my American Dream since becoming a father was sitting right across from me, asking me for some more time with his dad. A light went on in my head and I never looked back. Without a fallback plan, I said goodbye to telecom and hello to whatever job would have me close to home. At first, it was slim pickings. I delivered pizza, which I admit was more than humbling, having come from making about five to six times what a pizza delivery boy makes. I then took a second, slightly better job with a large hardware store where I supervised the night freight delivery team. I continued to put in long hours and for a lot less money, but working close to home and the predictable nature of my schedule allowed me to be more attentive to my son. I could go to school functions, coach his sports teams, watch his football games and truly relax with him on the weekends. Life was getting better for both of us and that elusive *dream* was becoming more of a reality.

After a year or so of that routine, financial problems once again reared their ugly head. Hard as I was working, I wasn't making enough money to cover all the bills, or give the government their due. For some reason, I was lured again to the plumbing trade. I knew from past experience that the money could be good and that jobs were readily available. However, I could not forget the painful and unpredictable schedule, which was not an option anymore. That's when I saw an ad in the paper for a small-business plumbing company, looking for an experienced plumber—that was me—who was interested in a growth opportunity. That sounded interesting, so I called the ad and set up an interview.

I'll never forget that first interview with the owner, Al Newell. He had been a Master Plumber for years and had a keen aptitude for business. His only question to me was if I had true and reliable aspirations to treat this job like a part owner and perhaps become full owner one day. That answer was easy. Heck yeah! My only question to him was would I be able to lead a normal life, have time for Joey at school functions, coach baseball and have weekends free. His answer was *yes*, with just one caveat. We would become a two-man team. So, he would cover for me when I needed my free time, so long as I covered for him when he needed his. He also assured me that he would teach me how to properly manage the business, both so that I might one day be able to take it over, but also so I could learn how avoid the insane time-consuming practices of our competitors that demanded the nutty schedules those poor guys had to keep. I have to tell you that this was the deal of a lifetime for me. Not only did I get to return to a trade that I thoroughly enjoyed, but it paid significantly better than anything else I was doing, and I had a legitimate shot at the American Dream of one day owning my own business.

The great irony of pursuing the American Dream in this country is the unpredictability of life on God's earth. When I got married, my vision of the American Dream had been a long and distinguished career in the military, sometime during which I would buy a farm for raising a large family. I had envisioned acres with animals, growing things, clearing land, digging holes and chopping wood with my son. In spite of that vision, I became a plumber, got divorced, spent years trying to regain my right to be a fulltime father to my son, and found myself working from the ground up repeatedly. I could never have dreamed of this future when I was a boy. Laying out in distant fields and gazing up at the glistening stars in the cool dark of night, truly I had a finer vision of the life I would lead.

Reflecting on my commitment to my son rekindles memories I had as a boy. As I share these memories and the various travails of my life with you, I think about what awaits my boy when he reaches adulthood. Perhaps it is naïve, but I don't want him to wake up in twenty years and wonder what happened. I don't want him to look back on his boyhood aspirations and be overwhelmed with a sense of regret. No one can know what challenges will come your way, or how they will ultimately shape your life. Yet, what happens to our country when we have successfully stamped out the drive and ambition of our youth? I tell you now without a doubt in my mind, my heart and my soul that the dreams of our youth are no less than God-given. Let us not tell our children that *dreams* are childish and wasteful things, for they are the building blocks of the American Dream. In my view, when we have paid our various dues in life, one way or another, we come back to those childhood fantasies. At some point, I think many of us, if we have played our cards right, get an opportunity to realize some measure of our grand schemes. In fact, if you think about your American Dream as a child, it wasn't about the big house, the fancy car, or all the toys in your closet. It was about being outside and enjoying God's good earth. It was about sunny weekends, the swimming hole, playing games on green fields, hot apple pie steaming from the oven, Thanksgiving feasts and the smell of Christmas pine. It doesn't matter how much money you make. So long as we preserve and defend our freedoms in this country, those days will be many. They will be accessible for any in this country who become wise enough to forget what they have learned and return to their youthful inexperience. Sound like pie in the sky? I sure hope so, because the further I have been from those childhood dreams, the less fun in life I was having. In fact, if you think about it, what value to life is there if you don't spend a great deal of your time enjoying it?

7

Finding My Faith

My dad's most common refrain when I was misbehaving as a boy was *God hates liars, cheaters and thieves.* Some of you may argue that God doesn't hate, but that wasn't the point he was trying to make. He wanted me to understand that such things were more than an abomination to each other on this earth; they are an affront to God. They were decried in the *Ten Commandments*, because lying, cheating and thieving ruins lives. Even if you are an atheist, you can't argue the wisdom in that. Where our earthly concerns alone are not enough to keep some of us in check, we must fear the judgment of something higher. That awful feeling I had as a young boy when I broke the scissors, wasn't some greater consciousness of my own. If it had been, then why didn't I feel it countless times before as I disrespected those around me, as well as myself? That sense of responsibility, which I couldn't shake, ate at something far deeper than the mind. I felt it deep in my gut. It resided in a place no instrument of man could reach. Though I knew it not at the time, that terrible feeling was my discovery of the spirit of the Lord inside me, and my pain was His moral judgment.

As a child growing up, church was a sporadic habit and never really a commitment. You see, we went through the motions of *faith*, but we really didn't make that leap from believing in God to embracing Him. Even my dad, who was clearly guided by God in good moral judgment and had stood as an extremely positive influence in my family, had not made the internal discovery that we all must make to truly become saved.

I suspect many of you reading this may be saying to yourselves, *Amen brother, hallelujah!* Others among you might be discovering something and thinking, *Wow, maybe I need to rethink my devotion to God and the meaning of faith.* Then there are those of you who are crying foul, saying, *Uh oh, here comes another rightwing whacko!* Regardless of your point of view, I am who I am, and I know my own heart and soul. As you have come to know something about me through the media and more so through these pages, I call it like I see it. I wasn't put on this earth to preach, but perhaps I am here to be that refreshing plainspoken voice we seldom hear anymore.

Throughout my life, I've been presented with a great many challenges, the likes of which have ruined other folks. They may shrivel up into a hole, which I almost did, or might become the product of the hated thing that hurt them. That could have also happened to me. However, I am a firm believer that at some point during our lives, God reaches out to us. It may happen while we are young or not until we grow old, but we must recognize the moment when it happens. Life on this planet is short, but everlasting life—well, is everlasting.

I don't believe in a set destiny for people. That goes against free will. What I do believe in are trials and consequences. At various points all throughout my life I have arrived at various crossroads. Upon reaching these junctures, I was presented with a choice, either to take the way to the left or turn to the right. Sometimes that left turn looked a lot smoother than the *right,* but it sure didn't prove to be. The times I did take the *right way,* though bumpy and rough, and with a few flat tires along the way, it proved to be the better route. The more practice I got in taking those *right turns* the smoother they began to look. The more often I reached the ends of those roads and realized how gratifying a journey it had been, the easier it became to choose that path. It's not something that happens overnight. It takes years of practice and dedication. So, when this 2008 election experience came my way, and I was approached with all sorts of *left turns,* I was able to recognize those temptations and turn myself *right.*

After the experience with the scissors when I was just ten years old, it took another five years before I reached the next crossroads. As it turned out, the rest of my family made the journey with me. We had moved back to Toledo, Ohio, the place where I was born, and into a house that is still in the family today and a not more than a block around the corner from where I presently live. After a year of making a new life in the North, we hadn't latched onto a church. It just hadn't been a priority. That changed when my brother Bobby began dating a girl who belonged to a church youth group. This girlfriend of his lured him into church with her on a fairly frequent basis, and he liked it. He would come home after a service and talk about it. This got the rest of the family to thinking about reengaging church and God, yet least of all me. It just so happened that I was pretty happy with my life, my school, my friends and my ability to sleep in late on Sunday mornings.

Nonetheless, as it was so often throughout my young life, Dad set the tone and made the key decisions for our family. He liked what he saw in Bobby's newfound enthusiasm for spiritual matters. As a result, he began to speak about the need for the family to get back to church as well. Dad was always a decisive man, so not more than a week went by when he insisted we all get our butts out of bed early on Sunday and get out to church to worship. As usual, I was stubborn and resisted at first, but I succumbed to a similar curiosity growing inside of me about religion.

As we renewed our habit of attending Sunday services and I attended Sunday school with Bobby, I began studying the various religions. This was how my dad had raised me, to get educated and to become informed before drawing conclusions. Sound familiar? For me, religion was no different. I had a basic belief in God, but I really knew little about what distinguished so many varying religions, which all claimed to be Christian in origin. For that matter, why wasn't there just a church of Christianity?

I began to read all I could on the subject of religion. I explored Jehovah's Witness, Catholicism, Protestantism, Baptists, Lutherans, Mormons . . . you name it, and I researched it as thoroughly as my normal school studies would allow. My conclusions were that they all held the same core beliefs, with the exception of ritualistic differences and some other idiosyncrasies. However, the fact that there were so many variations of faith caused me to look to science as well. I wanted proof of fact to understand the proper religious route to take, even if that meant abandoning religion as a whole.

Every Sunday after the service, I would take my arsenal of scientific data to my Sunday school class and impetuously engage my youth pastor in debate. His name was Monte McCune. Perhaps he will tell his story another time, but it is a testament to the greatness of God. I owe Monte my life. I don't think anyone else on earth, including my dad, could quite get through to me the way he did. He never shied from my peppering questions, and always had the perfect answer. He kept me guessing and searching for truth. As I learned later, my challenges were refreshing to him, amidst an otherwise disinterested class. Before meeting me, he had begun to question his calling, wondering if he was really making a difference. He ultimately made a big difference in my life, and succeeded in bringing me to terms with the emotions that ten-year-old boy felt that day with a pair of broken scissors in hand.

After months upon months of Sunday science versus religion debating sessions, Monte decided it was time to challenge me to the ultimate smack-down event. He asked me to meet him at the local Big Boy restaurant and to bring my science book from school. I had grown fond of him and so I accepted without hesitation. He advised that he would bring his Bible with him and that I could take him to task, point by point until I was satisfied I had proved science was superior to religion. How could I pass that up?

I met Monte at the Big Boy restaurant and sat with him in a booth. We ordered a couple of sodas and then he asked me to show him my science book. I pulled it out and put it on the table and then he pulled out his Bible and put it on the table next to the science book. They were each about equal thickness and chock-full of their own stories, lessons and supporting data. Of course, I believed at the time that my science book was superior, because it was based upon fact. The Bible, while interesting and compelling, was based upon belief, with little fact to support it.

Monte then took a deep breath and I braced myself for the ultimate showdown of Wurzelbacher science versus Monte's scripture. However, his first move was unexpected. He said, "Do me a favor and pick up your science book and read to me the first words at the top."

Puzzled, I picked up the book, studied it briefly and read, "Revised Edition Eight."

He nodded thoughtfully and then said, "Now pick up the Bible and read what it says."

I did as he said and read aloud, "The Holy Bible."

Monte leaned forward and looked me in the eye. "Do you see anything that says revised, Joe?"

He needed say nothing more. It hit me like a ton of bricks. I might have been dense, but I was plenty smart enough to understand the significance.

Monte gave me a moment, no doubt seeing my change of heart. At the very least, some small measure of the enormous eruption within my soul must have been evident. Finally he said, "You see Joe, man is always learning. Men will write what they learn, but will often have to revise their conclusions as they learn better. Sometimes, what they initially thought was true, isn't anymore. That's why you see a *Revised Edition* on your book, but not on the Bible. Next year, your school will introduce *Revised Edition Nine* while this book here," he pointed to the Bible I still held squarely in my hands, "will always be *The Holy Bible.* You can open it and read it cover to cover, but you will not see the word *revised*. The word of God needs no revision."

From that day forward I knew there was a God and felt no further need to question it. I loved Monte then and will forever for his time, effort and dedication to show me that truth. The Lord has been my rock ever since. As for Monte, I would learn years later that my discovery at that moment was also a turning point for him. It ironically reaffirmed to Monte his purpose on this earth. He eventually became a pastor of his own church. When he saw me all over the news, answering questions and then being chastised by the media and various leftwing organizations, he wrote me. He addressed his letter to "Joe the Christian Plumber." Monte, if ever you get an opportunity to read this book, I owe so much of what I am today to you. God bless you brother, I will always be a Christian no matter what else I do in life.

Church alone is not enough folks. You must have *faith*. Strength in belief, choosing the right path, avoiding and denying temptations all depend upon it. You can know everything there is to know about the Bible, you can memorize it word-for-word, but you will still fail without *faith*. Let me tell you also that *faith* isn't a destination, it's a journey fraught with peril and numerous challenges. I had discovered my *faith*, but it didn't mean I was a perfect angel from that point forward. It also didn't mean I had nothing yet to learn about the Lord's will and His purpose for me on this earth. Today as I share these things with you, I am still learning, mainly about purpose. Whenever you think you have it all figured out, here comes another curveball. Forgive the baseball analogy, but if you pull out of the batter's box, then you just might strike out. Instead, you have to dig in and wait for it to break. If your timing is right, you could hit the ball out of the park.

The next major lesson in my life was to learn that God is in charge and you are not. If you think you are in control, then you are sorely mistaken and downright delusional. Don't believe me? Just wait, you're time will eventually come. I just hope you don't have to learn it the hard way like I did, although you already know my affinity for hard lessons.

As you know, my marriage to Joey's mom didn't turn out like the fairytale story I had envisioned. Somehow, I figured that when you fall in love, the rest takes care of itself. After marriage, you make a home together, you have children, you work hard to provide for your family, you raise your children, you grow old, have grandchildren and hopefully, when the time comes, you have lived your life right and you have made a place for yourself in heaven, right? Evidently, I missed something in my equation for a perfect life. Being divorced has been one of the hardest things for me to admit to people. Frankly, I am ashamed of it. It feels like a failure of the highest degree, principally where children are concerned. The reality of my son being the product of a failed marriage hurts, and bothers me deeply. He didn't ask to be brought into this world, and yet his mother and I did just that.

Unfortunately, my divorce and the subsequent tug-o-war between my ex-wife and I for our son's custody is all too typical in America today. We have all heard the sad statistics that nearly one-half of all marriages end in divorce in this country, as well as in most other places in the modernized world. It makes you wonder if advanced society is really all that better. Regardless, when a union between a man and a woman results in offspring, it is incumbent upon the parents to put the interests of their children first. Ideally, this means that both parents put their self-interests aside until their children are grown. Often, however, either one or both of the parents do not. Which one might you be, the selfless or the selfish? Speaking firsthand, you can't control other people, least of all your *ex*. You can only do what you know to be right, and sometimes that means making sacrifices to accommodate the selfishness of the other half that produced your children. Sorry, but that's just the way it is. If you go around making excuses about how your *ex* has made it impossible for you to fulfill your responsibilities as a parent, then you are wrong and need to make an immediate adjustment. Our children need us, and particularly us fathers as they grow older. If you are not going to make the personal sacrifice, who will?

The fact that my son is the product of a failed marriage breaks my heart, but from the beginning I was determined to remain a staple in his life. There were a number of years where my *faith* in my pursuit of that duty and ideal lay in question. I cannot count how many times I prayed to God throughout that period of my life, begging Him to basically correct my mistakes for me. That was another harsh lesson. You have to live with your errors. Once you take that *left road,* there is no turning back. You have to follow it until you get to your next crossroad.

So what was my big mistake? Part of my problem is that I desperately sought and needed female attention. Sounds normal for a guy, right? However, I have learned throughout the years and by making plenty of mistakes that few things in the extreme are good. I lacked the balance to choose a wife with whom I was compatible for the long haul. I suppose she made the same mistake with me. I was committed, regardless of my poor choice, to make it work. Unfortunately, I underestimated just how important it is that both the man and the woman in the marriage share that commitment.

Growing up, I always had a problem with telling people I loved them. The only ones in my life with which I did not have that problem were my dogs. I suppose that's because a dog doesn't have a problem showing unmitigated affection. Scratch a dog's ear and he'll lick your face. Pat his back and he'll curl up next to you wherever you lay. Give him food and water and he'll . . . well I guess that's one drawback. You have to train a dog to do their business outside. However, once you've got that nicked everything else works out great.

The point is, relationships with people are a bit more complex. I hear you. *Of course they are, knucklehead!* I suppose I could blame this problem of mine on my childhood, the man that abandoned me, or a host of other negative occurrences in my life, but that would be a cop-out. In truth, we have only ourselves to blame for our poor decisions and bad actions.

As I have explained, elements of the media and Liberal political operatives sifted through the archives of my personal past and came up with a story that I was a wife-beater. As I have already explained, that is unequivocally NOT TRUE! I absolutely despise men who batter women. I learned the effects of a wife-beater at a very young age. Need I say more? Yes, I am angry about those B.S. accusations and I am going to hold those people to account, so help me.

The truth about the matter of my divorce is that my ex-wife and I simply weren't a good fit, and yet we had a son. Our mutual love for Joey was, I suppose, the primary catalyst for our custody dispute over him. After my childhood and having been abandoned, there was NO WAY I was going to ditch my son. It just wasn't gonna happen. The day of my son's birth was the most emotional, spiritual, awe-inspiring day of my life. Every priority and the totality of meaning in my life changed from that day forward. I WAS A FATHER! Nothing was ever going to change that, not even divorce.

Although I had inevitably become part of one sad statistic, I was not going to join the other group. Some sources estimate that nearly half of all children of divorced parents never see their father again after the divorce. HALF! Can you believe that? Listen brothers, if you are reading this and support me in everything else, but you belong to that *half* that didn't fight to remain a part of your kids' lives, then you've got some explaining to do. I don't care what the excuse, you have to do better. Children need a father. God didn't require the unique union between a man and a woman to create life just to see either one of them later ditch the scene. Listen, I know the statistics about court leanings in custody cases, and I know how difficult the path is to remaining in your child's life, but it's no excuse. I fought and I suffered for years, but eventually I succeeded in keeping my title of DAD. You can too!

Once again, it boils down to *faith*. I absolutely loved living in Alaska. As I've described, it was everything I dreamt it would be. Nonetheless, my wife wasn't happy there, and it wasn't my place to force her to be. Explain to me just how you make it so that someone comes to like something they just plain don't? When it became clear that no matter where we moved, the problem was more about *us* and not where we lived, we ultimately went down the path of divorce. As is often the case in America, she was granted custody of Joey. During this time, she had also decided to move to Arizona. It was every bit her right to live where she desired. It was also every bit my responsibility to follow her to make sure I remained a figure in my son's life. That is exactly what I did.

In total, I worked nine long hard years to keep being my son's dad. Those years I lived in Arizona were the toughest. Nothing against the state or the people, but I really didn't like it there. It just wasn't home and the relationship between my ex-wife and I had not yet evolved to a place where we could agree to set our differences aside for the benefit of our son. Thus, I was alone in a strange land, suddenly living a life I had never imagined would be mine. Basically, I worked and I fought for custody of Joey. That was it! In the little spare time I had, when I wasn't allowed to be with my son, I worked out in the gym, I studied the Bible and I prayed to God for deliverance.

Do you know what it takes to prove to an American court that you're fit to be dad, even when you've done nothing wrong? As crazy as that sounds, it's a reality for a lot of dads out there, as it was for me. The first thing you have to do is forget about saving money or having anything of value. As I already mentioned, every dime I had went towards child support and legal expenses. If you are committed to being a father, then you have no choice. As such, I went deep into debt. I forwent the creature comforts of life. I didn't buy *things,* I didn't go out, I didn't date and I didn't indulge in anything. Eventually, I also forgot about paying taxes to the government. Yep, *Joe the Tax Evader* decided it was better to spend that money on sustaining my presence in my son's life. I wonder how God will judge me for that? It's not like the government was ever going to forgive me for that debt. I knew eventually I'd have to pay up. I have and will continue to pay the government their due, but I wonder if ever there was a more justifiable cause for the government to give tax relief than for a father's fight to remain a fixture in his child's life. Perhaps a great many evils in this country would not come into being if more of us made sacrifices to be dads.

Throughout those long and trying years as a weekend dad, all that I was missing in Joey's life constantly haunted me. It wasn't some emotion in my mind, it was a deep hurt down in the far reaches of my soul. Every man feels it for his child, even those who abandon their children and over time learn to ignore it. I often wondered if I would ever get to be an influential part of his childhood. Was I living a life of misery and financial destitution for nothing? Without *faith* I would have abandoned my path and taken any one of the many *left turns* that came my way. Instead, I cleaved to my faith in God and I continued to pray that sometime soon my hard work and dedication would pay off.

As it turned out, my prayers were eventually answered. It didn't happen soon or according to any mental timeline I could conceive. My reunion with my boy came when that next *right turn* came my way. Despite many years of battling things out in court, my ex-wife and I at last reconciled for the sake of our son. Joey came to live with me for the first time in nine long years. In many ways he was all grown up, but he still needed and continues to need a father. There has been no greater blessing in my life than this opportunity I have been given to see him grow into a man. Thanks to God, I hung on when I felt I couldn't go on any longer, and now I'm living my particular American Dream.

You may ask yourself, why would I wish to tell this story and share such personal aspects of my life. In truth, I am fast getting over my discomfort with having to share myself with America. A combination of politicians and media didn't give me much of a choice. However, the greater reason is that I fear for the future of our country where the word *God*, much less the *word of God,* has become more offensive than any profane word that has been invented. Think about that for a second. Protesters can march right down Main Street U.S.A. anywhere in this country, half-naked, cursing up a storm, burning American flags and just about anything else, and without limitation or consequence. In fact, these displays of supposed *Free Speech* are often celebrated widely amongst the media. Yet, when just one man comes out into the public square and whispers *God,* one might think the British were once again marching through the streets of Boston. Why is that?

I suspect many of you are just as fed up with the supposed *Separation of Church and state* clause, which appears nowhere in our Constitution, as I am. If you believe there is such a clause, then shame on you, you haven't read perhaps the second-most important document in history, next to the Bible. If you assumed there was such a clause or accepted the opinions of the many voices spoken through or as a part of the media, then once again, shame on you. Put down this book and read the Constitution before you continue on. You can find it on the Internet, at your local library or in a number of books at the bookstore. Read it all and reread it often. The only reason why this book was available for your reading pleasure, is that a group of exceptionally wise men decided to put their lives and all that they held dear at stake for the future of our country and all the generations that would be born on this soil or come here in search of the American Dream.

Now that you have read it, you now know that the Constitution makes only one reference concerning laws about religion. It is a part of the Bill of Rights, and the first of ten constitutional amendments, fathered by George Mason IV and James Madison. It reads as follows:

AMENDEMENT I
Congress shall make no law respecting an establishment of <u>religion</u>, or prohibiting the free exercise thereof; or abridging the freedom of speech, or of the press; or the right of the people peaceably to assemble, and to petition the Government for a redress of grievances.

So there it is in black and white. Reads like simple English to me. Does is not to you? There is no *separation of church and state.* It only says that *Congress shall make no law respecting an establishment of religion.* You don't have to know why this was so important to the colonials to understand the meaning, but it can clear up some assertions made by many a lawyer in an effort to confound the ideals and beliefs of our Founding Fathers. Fact is, the Founding Fathers, and specifically men like George Mason IV feared the kind of religious persecution that had plagued Europe for centuries. Don't you find it ironic that today the ACLU and various other anti-American organizations have used Mason's own First Amendment language for the persecution of the Christian faith—the absolute antithesis of its intended purpose?

If you find this a little, or a lot, over the edge, then consider the court-ordered removal of the granite monument displaying the *Ten Commandments* within the rotunda of the Alabama State Judicial Building in 2003. Didn't you know about this case? Look it up and learn about the victory of the ACLU and their minions over average everyday Americans who supported Judge Roy Moore in vast, overwhelming numbers. The enlightened higher courts in this case *(please!)* cited that the monument established a *"permanent recognition of the 'sovereignty of God,' the Judeo-Christian God, over all citizens in this country . . ."* Judge Moore was subsequently removed from office as a result of his defense of the monument. The Alabama Court of the Judiciary found that he had violated the *Canons of Ethics.* To this, Moore adroitly replied, *"To acknowledge God cannot be a violation of the Canons of Ethics. Without God there can be no ethics."* Sounds like common sense to me. How about you?

This legal fight epitomizes the dire nature of this country's identity crisis. What's wrong with having a display of the *Ten Commandments* on public land and in public view? Are the laws of this nation not based upon those ten pinnacles of the Judeo-Christian faith? What is so repugnant among them that they should be removed? No one said, "Swear to this stone monument that you are devoted to a Judeo-Christian faith or *we the court* will judge thee unfairly." Even the Preamble of the State's constitution contains the words:

*We, the people of the State of Alabama, in order to establish justice, insure domestic tranquility, and secure the blessings of liberty to ourselves and our posterity, invoking the favor and guidance of **__Almighty God__** . . .*

Furthermore, Moses and the *Ten Commandments* are depicted all throughout Washington D.C., in the rotunda of the Library of Congress, on the Supreme Court Building and in their courtroom, and the list goes on. Shall all these monuments be removed? Should the words *this nation, under God* etched into the walls of the Lincoln Monument, citing Abraham Lincoln's Gettysburg Address be chiseled clean? Where has all common sense in this country gone?

I'll answer that, because it's not the common sense of the average American that has failed, it is primarily the courts and the anti-God, anti-capitalism and anti-American Dream legions that guide them. Make no mistake, we are living in the midst of an oligarchy, primarily superseded by the judiciary. What does that mean? It means we live in a country founded as a democratic Republic, a nation ruled by the people's elected representatives, but those representatives don't appear to be representing us. Those rare officials that do, are too often thwarted by the courts with impunity.

Getting back to my main point, God is in jeopardy of being ousted from the United States of America, if He doesn't decide to leave us beforehand. Okay, maybe it's just the Christian God, but how in the world does a country of nearly 80% Christians allow that to happen? Remember that Edmund Burke quote? Let me jog your memory . . .

"All that is necessary for the triumph of evil in America is for good men (and women) to do nothing."

Okay, I added the *women* part, but ladies you all are in this fight too. And why are we losing this battle for American Values? We are losing, because we are too complacent. We have become too absorbed in the comforts of our homes, our televisions, cars, vacations, restaurants, shopping . . . don't you see it?

Some of you may ask, "What's so important about God?" Those more moderate may say, "Having God in the courthouse isn't going to strengthen my faith or anyone else's." I am inclined to agree with the latter, but we would all be missing the larger picture. If you find yourself lost about now, go back and reread this chapter and pay closer attention to my life's lessons in the beginning. Joe the boy was in danger of becoming Joe the adult criminal, or worse. Joe the boy didn't have the capacity to correct himself. Why? Because the human intellect is weak. We are a people predominantly driven by desire. Moral reckoning is not human nature. If you think it is, then I challenge you to prove it. History, whether ancient or contemporary, has surely rendered firm judgment on that point.

Let me give you an example of the fallacy of those who cling to *separation of church and state* as an honorable means to preserve religious freedom in our country. You ready? Here you go . . . Does the concept of *freedom of religion* equally apply to satanism? Do any of you have an idea what the worship of the ultimate evil involves? Shall the government of the United States of America, of *We The People,* have no ground by which to prohibit such activity?

The truth is, our Founding Fathers believed in God, and made God's Law inherent in the laws of this nation. They could never have stomached how the First Amendment has been abused by those who oppose God. How could anyone oppose God? Our country was founded on the principle that God's blessings are essential to the life and security of a nation and its people. Now if you disagree with that, you have been given that *right* by the very same Amendment. However, that *right* never extended to limiting the rights of those who wish to worship God. Moreover, if you don't believe there is a God, then why would you care? How does letting the vast majority of America have our illusions harm you? There can be only one logical answer to that question, given all the protections of citizens under the Constitution and Bill of Rights. If ever you discover that reason, then God help you if you don't see the light.

8

What I Look For In A President

During Obama versus McCain I, II, and III, if you weren't falling asleep or throwing something at the television screen, then check your pulse, because you just might be dead. Am I the only one who wanted these two men in a contest for the most powerful office in the world to take off the gloves and have at it? Of course, I'm not suggesting they should have lunged at each others' throats, but couldn't these opponents at least have looked each other in the eye and addressed each other directly? I'm not the least bit interested in genteel candidates and their mutual respect for each other. I want cage warfare, flying wingtips, torn Armani and silk socks slinging cufflinks! Does that make me a bad guy?

One of the things, among many, that disturb me most about politics today is that it has become a celebrity contest. Sure, popularity is always important, but since when did a presidential candidate need to compete with the Hollywood Elite?

When I was in school, I never cared for fads or status symbols. I wore flannel shirts, cowboy boots and listened to country music long before such things were remotely cool. No, I didn't go to school in Nashville, or some other country-ville area. I may have fit in better or had more to relate to, but my parents lived in Toledo Ohio. The point is not that Country Music is better than Hip-Hop (I like both), nor is it that boots are better than hi-tops or loafers. I am certainly not making a case for *Joe The President 2012*. Don't even start! What I'm trying to say is that there is something profoundly refreshing about an individual that makes no excuses for who they are and offers their true opinions without first checking in with a focus group. When was the last time we had an unrepentant politician who would sooner fall on his or her sword than compromise principles?

I can hear the howls from the Ivy League, collegiate elite, Why don't you call yourself Joe the Idiot? Telling the truth will never work! Obama told people what they wanted to hear and he won by a landslide! Duh!

Perhaps they're right, but I never did try to fit in and flock with the crowd. My impression of Governor Palin is that she was cut from that same cloth, and no, she won't be spending the majority of her year away from home fighting the good fight on Capitol Hill. That's probably good for her and her family, though she was willing to make the sacrifice.

Before having met Obama in my neighborhood, I would never have presumed that anyone would care what Joe Wurzelbacher admired in a President of the United States. However, given what happened thereafter and all the outpouring of support, and condemnation since, I thought perhaps I should share with you what I seek in a presidential candidate every election year, but have yet to find.

From the annals of American History, there are three presidents that for me rise high above the rest. These men epitomized the unique qualities of being American, but also stand out for their morals, values, and invaluable contributions to the future of our country. Their greatness can only be measured by the long shadows they have cast over the few men who have risen to the unique office of the Presidency, whether before or since. Theirs is the yardstick by which all presidents are measured, and justifiably so.

George Washington
(President 1789 – 1797)

I suppose this is an obvious choice, but George Washington was a giant of a man, not just in physical stature, but also as a statesman. Naturally, I will have nothing to say about the man beyond what has already been recorded by historians for over two centuries, but I can share those attributes of his that I admire the most.

I have no child for whom I could wish to make a provision – no family to build in greatness upon my country's ruins.

—George Washington

Washington is often hailed as one of our greatest presidents, if not the greatest. I think this is fair, considering his role in establishing both the country and a presidency, as opposed to a monarchy. Some historians have judged his military prowess harshly, but I think the results speak for themselves. He took a disorganized and fragmented army of disparate colonies and defeated the greatest military power the world had yet seen. If that's not convincing enough, I don't know what would be.

Perhaps Washington's greatest qualities were his limited to non-existent ego, and profound devotion to the service of his fellow man. When given the opportunity to become a monarch after the war, he flatly refused. Can you say WOW! In fact, when the war had ended, Washington had every intention of retiring to his home on Mount Vernon. When King George III heard of this, he remarked, *"If he does that, he will be the greatest man in the world!"*

Having similar admiration for Washington, Napoleon evidently kept a bust of Washington on his desk and ordered a day of mourning for him upon his passing. Later, while in exile, Napoleon would write of his fondness for Washington's wisdom, discipline and pure lack of interest for power. Napoleon expressed regret that he didn't possess Washington's ability to ignore the temptation for power. Is there a politician today you can honestly say would pass up being king, if just for a day?

Government is not reason, it is not eloquence, it is force. Like fire, it is a dangerous servant and a fearful master.
—*George Washington*

Washington would naturally become the model for all presidents that would follow his terms in office. If only more of them could have shared his distaste for partisan political agendas and put the honest interests of *We The People* first, perhaps the city bearing his name would also have sustained his character and integrity. Washington believed that party loyalty would ultimately lead to the rise of an oppressive government and the ruination of our individual freedoms. He cited the lessons of history as a means to convey the oppressive nature of unwieldy government. In his farewell address, he keenly focused on a belief that *sooner or later the chief of some prevailing faction* would rise to power and be the instrument through which our *Public Liberty* would be undone. Why? Washington wisely understood that human nature is to prop up one group of people who share one set of ideals or interests at the expense of all who do not.

Guard against the impostures of pretended patriotism.
—*George Washington*

Thomas Jefferson once described Washington in memoriam as being *incapable of fear, meeting personal dangers with the calmest unconcern.* This must have been especially inspiring to Washington's men during the Revolutionary War and probably meant the difference between victory and defeat against Britain. I have said it in interviews, but I really like the idea of a former military commander being President and Commander-in-Chief. As one who will be in a position to make war for the defense of our country, I think it helps for our president to understand firsthand what it means to lead our military men and women, as well as to know the horrors of war up close and personal. How else can one make a sound judgment that may lead to incalculable death and destruction?

Above all, Washington believed in service to his countrymen and the inimitable virtue of sacrifice. He feared for the preservation of freedom in America and understood that our Constitutional Rights are key to ensuring its resilience. He also attempted to teach us all that the greatest threat to our Constitutional freedoms would come by those from within who would use words like *patriotism* and *freedom*, not for the benefit of *We The People*, but for self-interest and political power.

Abraham Lincoln
(President 1861 – 1865)

Again, no surprises, I can recognize greatness just as well as the next guy. Lincoln is always ranked among the best due to his monumental accomplishment of restoring the Union. Had he failed, I'm not sure anyone could objectively argue our great country would exist today. Just think of the challenges that we have faced since his term in office, not to mention the desperate struggles against tyranny throughout the world. Would a divided America have been able to overcome the Axis during World War II?

Don't interfere with anything in the Constitution. That must be maintained, for it is the only safeguard of our liberties.

—Abraham Lincoln

Like Washington before him, Lincoln believed in the sanctity of our Constitution and the rights it conveyed to the American people. Again, like Washington, he also realized that the greatest threat to our nation would come from within our borders. He had undoubtedly witnessed this force with the onset of the Civil War.

In his Gettysburg Address, Lincoln spoke of *a new birth of freedom* finally realized from the initial drafting of our Constitution. Though brief, this speech has been hailed among the greatest of all time, and speaks to his belief in the unique foresight of our Founding Fathers. I don't think it was an accident that the forgers of the Constitution omitted any specific racial reference to inalienable rights. These men were some of the brightest minds in history, and clearly had an eye for the future. Lincoln espoused this belief as well.

I know that the Lord is always on the side of the right. But it is my constant anxiety and prayer that I and this nation should be on the Lord's side.
—Abraham Lincoln

Aside from the tremendous test of Lincoln's ability to lead during the Civil War, I most admire his evolving concept of God as it pertained to the blessings of our country. When a clergyman once commented to Lincoln regarding the Civil War, *"I hope the Lord is on our side."* Lincoln's response (above) was poignant as usual, but also spoke to his complex view of religion as it pertained to the peril of our country.

I doubt another president has ever experienced more tragedy or felt the burden of office greater. He and his wife had four sons, yet only one survived into adulthood. One of his sons died of typhoid fever in the White House amidst numerous setbacks in the war against the South. I can't imagine a greater test of a man's soul and commitment to faith than this. How Lincoln remained strong for the country in spite of the worst and most painful kind of personal tragedy is beyond me. Like many things, I suppose when you're thrust into the midst of such circumstances, you have only two choices. History would prove that Lincoln took the *right road.*

Both read the same Bible, and pray to the same God; and each invokes His aid against the other. It may seem strange that any men should dare to ask a just God's assistance in wringing their bread from the sweat of other men's faces; but let us judge not that we be not judged. The prayers of both could not be answered; that of neither has been answered fully. The Almighty has his own purposes. "Woe unto the world because of offences! for it must

needs be that offences come; but woe to that man by whom the offence
cometh!" If we shall suppose that American Slavery is one of those offences
which, in the providence of God, must needs come, but which, having
continued through His appointed time, He now wills to remove, and that He
gives to both North and South, this terrible war, as the woe due to those by
whom the offence came, shall we discern therein any departure from those
divine attributes which the believers in a Living God always ascribe to Him?
Fondly do we hope—fervently do we pray—that this mighty scourge of war
may speedily pass away. Yet, if God wills that it continue, until all the
wealth piled by the bond-man's two hundred and fifty years of unrequited
toil shall be sunk, and until every drop of blood drawn with the lash, shall be
paid by another drawn with the sword, as was said three thousand years ago,
so still it must be said "the judgments of the Lord, are true and righteous
altogether."

—Abraham Lincoln, part of his Second Inaugural Address

The mere election of the nation's first Republican President, Abraham Lincoln, had resulted in the secession of the South. The
Republican Party had been founded in opposition to slavery, the
South's primary economic engine, and the South had little doubt
about Lincoln's long-term goals. Despite any political olive branches
extended to them, the South believed in their States' Rights to
preserve an institution whose abolition would have destroyed their
economy. If the two sides could have come to agreement, Lincoln
most likely would not have opposed maintaining the status quo,
which meant slavery where it existed would be maintained, but
expansion would not be allowed. Naturally, during any conflict of
ideals, there is seldom any middle ground. Lincoln no doubt viewed
slavery as repugnant, but deemed it more of a philosophical issue
than moral. Where moral issues were determined by the Bible,
which set precedent for slavery, Lincoln's philosophical arguments
were grounded in the essence of our Constitution and Bill of Rights.
How could *all men are created equal* not apply to All Men?

No one knows exactly how Lincoln would have governed had
the South not seceded and taken its aggressive actions at Fort

Sumter. Personally, I think that although he abhorred the institution of slavery, he didn't believe it could be completely abolished without a great and costly conflict. No one wanted that, because it would only have served to weaken a budding nation. Nonetheless, at some point during the war, Lincoln seemed to realize that he had been swept up into events far greater in scope and meaning than his political career. He believed he had become, or perhaps had always been, a providential instrument of righting a great wrong.

On September 22, 1863, Lincoln issued an executive order, setting into motion the Emancipation Proclamation, thus bringing about an end to slavery and a realization of the American Dream first brought into focus by our Founding Fathers. A gifted orator and writer, Lincoln's sentiments regarding slavery, which he long kept under wraps for the sake of trying to keep the country together, were at last presented to the American people in the form of his second inaugural address on March 4, 1865. The thing I can't get past is how inspiring these words remain after nearly a century and a half. No politician writes or speaks this way anymore. Could you imagine if one came forth that did?

After four years of the absolute worst kind of torment anyone can ever imagine a president having during his term in office, Lincoln at last saw peace on the horizon as he prepared for his second inaugural address. It was a gray and entirely overcast day, yet the crowd was jubilant to hear their president. As Lincoln arose to deliver his speech, a sudden burst of sunlight broke through the clouds and illuminated the great man where he stood. It startled Lincoln, but he composed himself and proceeded to address the crowd with words that have been forever engraved in history, just as they are upon the walls of his monument in Washington D.C. The response from the gathered crowd was profound, for this was not a speech for which to cheer and offer frequent and unabated applause. Instead it was regarded with silent and tearful reflection.

The tragedy of Lincoln is that he never got to see the fruits of his labor, prayers and misery. As he gave that fateful speech, he was walking through the valley of the shadow of death. Like Washington before him, I think he was uniquely qualified for the times during which he served, and purposefully selected for the task at hand.

Theodore Roosevelt
(President 1901 – 1909)

My undisputed favorite president of all time is Theodore Roosevelt. My affinity for T.R., as his friends called him, stems from his love of nature, sense of adventure and quest for conservationism. He was also unafraid to challenge the greatest corporate giants of his time, a quality seemingly nonexistent in today's political scene.

Speak softly and carry a big stick . . .

—Theodore Roosevelt

T.R.'s famous *big stick* motto has become a staple in my own household. I view it as just plain brilliance. I try to emulate this principle in my own life and instill it in my son. It is a measure of an individual's self-confidence and yet steady apportionment of one's ability to enforce his or her will upon others.

The man who loves other countries as much as his own stands on a level with the man who loves other women as much as he loves his own wife.

The only man who is a good American is the man who is an American and nothing else.

—Theodore Roosevelt

These quotes speak to the heart of Washington and Lincoln's shared concerns that our nation will one day be torn asunder by forces from within. During a time when Irish and German immigrants' loyalties were divided over German aggression that would eventually lead to U.S. involvement in World War I, T.R. chastised the so-called *hyphenated Americans.* In T.R.'s view, they really weren't American at all. T.R. made it clear that he was not referring to *naturalized Americans* for whom he had great respect. Instead, he spoke of individuals who hail America as their home, yet do not consider the interests of America first, foremost and without equal to any land from which they may have originally come. He believed this was a profound internal danger to the very fabric of the United States. He feared that we would eventually become a society of squabbling nationalities. Look around you, watch the news and read a newspaper. Have we not become that nation? Is Barack Obama going to be inaugurated as our African-American President, or just our American President? What's wrong with just being American? I wonder if one day it will no longer be politically acceptable to identify oneself as American without a preceding *race, creed, color* or *origin* hyphen. Once being American has lost all its meaning, why bother?

The only man who makes no mistakes is the man who never does any-thing.

—*Theodore Roosevelt*

One of the things I like most about T.R. is that although he was born into a life of privilege, coming from a successful business family in New York and graduating an Ivy Leaguer from Harvard, he reinvented himself while exploring out West in North Dakota. He built a ranch there called Elkhorn and learned to be an adept horseman, to rope and to hunt. He became a deputy sheriff and on one occasion hunted down and captured three outlaws who made off with his riverboat, trying to escape up North. He didn't hang them, as was common in that day, but guarded them for forty tireless hours until he could get them to trial. During this period of his life, living in and exploring the Badlands of the Dakota Territory, he learned the value of a man's connection with nature. This would culminate into a conservation movement that continues today.

Among his various positions and trades, he authored *The Naval War of 1812*, considered the definitive history of the period's naval warfare at the time and after. He also wrote *The Winning of the West,* through which he propagated his views on America's destiny to settle and civilize the savage West. He was president of the American Historical Association, appointed to the United States Civil Service Commission, president of the board of New York City Police Commissioners, and Assistant Secretary of the Navy.

Wars are, of course, as a rule to be avoided; but they are far better than certain kinds of peace.

—*Theodore Roosevelt*

When the Spanish-American War broke out, T.R. resigned his naval secretary post in President McKinley's cabinet to join the army and take part in a fight for which he strongly believed. He became a lieutenant colonel and took command of his own regiment, called *The Rough Riders.* This is where I absolutely fell in love with T.R., as did the country at the time.

Already a popular and powerful figure, T.R. was initially offered full command of his own regiment, but he declined, as he had only served in the New York National Guard and felt he lacked the proper military experience. Instead, he deferred the honor to an associate of his and Medal of Honor winner, Colonel Leonard Wood. With an experienced commander at the head, T.R. set about the task of recruitment. He gathered together a wild and ragtag bunch of volunteers consisting of ranch-hands, cowboys, Ivy League athletes, Pawnee scouts and many others whom he primarily had come to know during his time in the Badlands of North Dakota and tenure as New York Police Commissioner. I don't know about you, but that sounds like my kind of crowd!

With his *Rough Riders* assembled, T.R. and company went down to San Antonio, Texas for a month of training, then moved on to Florida, where they awaited a boat to Cuba. However, what started out as a cavalry brigade quickly turned into an infantry fighting force when transportation issues caused them to leave most all their horses and a dozen of the volunteers behind. I guess we didn't exactly have our military act together back then, but we were willing and able, as T.R. adeptly proved.

The pinnacle of that conflict came at the *Battle of San Juan Hill*. T.R.'s personal heroism, in spite of the hesitancy among senior officers, carried the day. The American forces were pinned down suffering heavy casualties beneath the Spanish defensive position atop the hill. T.R. catalyzed a charge that ultimately succeeded in taking the hill and sent the Spaniards into retreat and eventual defeat. This action and successful victory propelled him into near unparalleled fame amongst Americans back home. He was later recommended for the Medal of Honor, but it was disapproved by military officials that were most likely singed by a *round robin letter* that T.R. sent to them regarding the dire condition of our soldiers in Cuba. In the letter, which somehow got leaked to the press, T.R. strongly implored the American commanders to essentially get off their butts and bring our soldiers back home! After succeeding in defeating the Spanish, malaria and other diseases were killing more of our men than had fallen in battle. Despite the self-serving notions of the military power structure back then, a renewed interest in T.R.'s heroism and service to his country brought him his just due in 2001 when President Clinton awarded T.R. the Congressional Medal of Honor posthumously. He is the first and only president in the history of our country to have received such an honor. Now that's a president I can get behind!

After his legendary heroics in the Spanish-American war, T.R. became governor of New York, then Vice President under William McKinley. When McKinley was assassinated only six-months into his second term by Leon Czolgosz, a reputed socialist and anarchist, T.R. was sworn-in as President of the United States.

If it wasn't for the high office I hold, I would have taken him by the seat of the breeches and the nape of the neck and chucked him out the window.
—Theodore Roosevelt

One of the legacies of T.R.'s presidency that I respect the most is his title of *Trust Buster*. Today, I can't think of a single politician that has vigorously taken on corporate greed. Forget about all the political propagandism from either party, who isn't in the hands of big corporations and Wall Street dealers anymore? T.R. wasn't about talk, he was about action for the benefit of regular Americans. He dismantled forty-four trusts. What was the benefit to the American people? Some would argue, but more competition in the marketplace breeds better quality and lower prices for us, regular Middle-American consumers. Can you think of an example of unmitigated corporate greed today? Let me give you one guess; they pump black stuff out of the earth.

During the Coal Strike of 1902, T.R. once again put the people first, this time against the interests of both the United Mine Workers of America and the coal mine owners. He believed that America, with a potentially devastating winter coming, could not and should not be held hostage by such disputes. He ultimately settled the dispute by forcing the middle ground both sides were too stubborn to find themselves. He held a special contempt for the corporate greed of the coal mine owners, and of one George Baer. Baer was the subject of T.R.'s *chuck out the window* remark. Can you see Clinton, Bush or Obama doing that to one of these oil barons today? How about Speaker Pelosi, Harry Reed or anyone else on Capitol Hill for that matter?

The great challenge for T.R. during this crisis was to not overstep the bounds of the power of the presidency, while preventing either polarized side of the issue from dragging our country into ruin. On the coal mine owners side you have unrepentant greed, the result of unchecked and amoral capitalism. On the coal union's side you have the threat of socialism, which is all about equal distribution of wealth and ultimately the death of the America Dream. Although T.R. vehemently opposed corporate greed, he readily acknowledged that our American Dream is fueled by individual enterprise and the pursuit of success through hard work and spirited competition. I think T.R. handled the situation well, as he looked out for the primary interests of the American people at large. However, these issues never stay resolved. Ask yourself what other presidents in history would have done in T.R.'s shoes and you just might find a chain of events that would have ultimately destroyed our country. Somehow, T.R. found the balance that was needed.

There can be no greater issue than that of conservation in this country.
                                                                —*Theodore Roosevelt*

Perhaps T.R.'s greatest legacy is his important and timely strides for the preservation of our natural resources and the stunning beauty of our land. He pushed Congress to establish the U.S. Forest Service, recognizing that without conservation techniques, our country would not only lose a vital natural resource, but also a number of its flora and fauna national treasures. A number of animal species had either gone extinct or were on the brink, including Bald Eagles, Buffalo, Black Bears, Grizzly Bears, Elk, Mountain Lions, Passenger Pigeons (already extinct), and the list goes on. He established hunting limitations and set aside an unprecedented 194 million acres of national parks and preserves, the results of which speak for themselves today. As an outdoor enthusiast, avid fisherman and occasional hunter, I am eternally grateful. Were it not for his decisive action, wisdom and forethought, much of what we enjoy about the outdoors in our country today would not be possible.

When I think of an ideal president of the greatest country on God's good earth, I reflect on men like Washington, Lincoln and T.R. I don't admire them because they were Presidents of the United States. I am inspired by their character, their greatness amidst adversity and their contributions for the sake of sustaining our American Dream. I wonder how long before their great accomplishments and precedents will be lost to our children. How much do our schools bother to teach about these pillars of American History these days? I think that is a fair question to ask in a country that no longer finds Washington and Lincoln worthy of their own days of honor, as their honorary birthdays were combined into Presidents' Day during Nixon's presidency as a means to honor all presidents. How many of you believe Nixon is entitled to the same honor as Washington and Lincoln? These days we celebrate Martin Luther King Day, whom I also believe was a great man. What's wrong with these giants of history each having their own day of honor? Is one more federal holiday going to grind this country to a screeching halt?

Perhaps more than anything else, I think great presidents hearken to the lessons of history and in times of crisis take frequent counsel with Almighty God. They understand that our liberties and our unique way of life are far from reproach, but that the greatest threat to our undoing is not from abroad, but from within.

President Reagan, whom I also greatly respect, shared this wisdom and understanding in perhaps finer words than any before him or since. I pray that wisdom continues to reverberate today and never ceases in the American consciousness throughout the ages.

Freedom is never more than one generation away from extinction. We didn't pass it to our children in the bloodstream. It must be fought for, protected, and handed on for them to do the same, or one day we will spend our sunset years telling our children and our children's children what it was once like in the United States where men were free.

—Ronald Reagan

9

Spreading The Wealth

I think when you spread the wealth around, it's good for everybody.
—Barack Obama 10/24/2008

Will this be the defining quote of our new president, or will it
fade into the many pre-election statements or missteps that have
often been forgotten by history. What truly matters from this point
on, is what President-elect Obama does going forward. I readily
acknowledge that candidates running for election for any public
office in this country since Washington have often found themselves
pandering to their listening audience. It is a sad, but true fact that
often we don't really know what a politician will do in office until
they are tested.

I have said it in interviews and I will repeat now that I am fearful
about the agenda of our new president. I pray that he succeeds in
strengthening our country and does not do it irreparable harm.
Many of you, regardless of party preference, voted for your *team.* If
you are among those who now want our president to personally fail,
and by doing so, drag the country down with him, then SHAME
ON YOU! As you hopefully now understand after reading the

previous chapter, presidents transcend politics. The good of the country, as Washington warned, has nothing to do with the success of a political party, but everything to do with you and me continuing to have the greatest driving force for success in the history of the world—The American Dream. *Spreading The Wealth,* by contrast, is a monumentally bad idea. I fear that Obama meant exactly what he said. I fear that I somehow caught him at a moment when his tremendous wordsmithing abilities were taking a smoke-break. Only time will tell.

At the chance that *Spreading The Wealth* will become a priority of Obama's first term, we must band together to oppose it. I don't care if you are a Democrat, Republican, Independent, Libertarian, Socialist—oh, well I guess if you belong to that party, this is exactly what you want.

I've been widely criticized by the media, pundits, Internet-hacks, political campaign operatives from both sides of the aisle and pretty much everyone besides the heart and soul of our country—YOU, for my comparisons of Obama's remarks to socialist-Marxist ideals. Okay, let me just come out and say again, IT IS SOCIALISM! It's irrefutable. Here's the Webster's definition again, in case you missed it earlier:

SOCIALISM
1. any of various theories or systems of the ownership and operation of the <u>means of production and distribution</u> by <u>society or the community</u> rather than by private individuals, with all members of society or the community sharing in the work and the products. **2.** a) <u>political movement</u> for establishing such a system b) the doctrines, methods, etc. of the Socialist parties. **3.** the stage of society, in <u>Marxist doctrine</u>, coming between the capitalist stage and the <u>communist stage</u>, in which private ownership of the <u>means of production and the distribution</u> has been eliminated.

Let's break this down and see if I'm the one who's lost it, or if the media and every other closet-socialist mouthpiece have. First, *means* is by definition, resources, capital, money, DOLLARS & CENTS. Don't be fooled by the term *society or the community,* because in the practical world of socialist (or communist) society, something or someone has to decide how the *means* are evenly distributed, and that is always going to be a GOVERNMENT. There is no other option. You can't crowd three hundred and fifty million people in a room to each grab their share of corn, bread, eggs, milk, cars, medicine, and everything else that comes with centralized apportionment of goods and services and expect everyone to play fair, can you? Of course not, but don't you see what this is really about? It is about supposed *fairness* enforced by government gunpoint. Sound too extreme? Just look up a little about the history of socialism, Marxism and communism. Wherever these ideals have been put into practice, countless lives have been destroyed, erased, wiped out, and you name it. Those that survived became slaves to a system over which they had no control. Sure, the idealism behind *fairness* sounds good, but in practice it goes against nature. Without exception, a revolution that chose a socialist system of government wound up with a less productive, less rewarding and ultimately a more punishing life than they had under the rule of a king or dictator. Don't believe me? Look it up! Here are some core examples: USSR, China, North Korea, Viet Nam and Cuba. If life is or was so great in these countries, then why do so many seek to flee from them to come to America? Because we have The American Dream. Why is it that people thousands of miles away understand this better than millions living in this country? Yes, we have to acknowledge that there are millions in this country, in fact, tens of millions that have been lulled into the false and altogether idiotic idea that socialist principles are better alternatives to capitalism. Deceptively, the Socialists in this country don't call it *socialism,* they call it *fairness, moral obligation, true Christianity, rights, justice, equality,* and in this election season I heard it many times called *Hope.*

Let me tell you my version of Hope. I *hope* that one day my son won't find that every bit of extra effort he puts into his vocation, his job or business or any pursuit in life isn't redistributed to all those who didn't care to put forth the extra effort. I *hope* that if he wants to work harder, become more educated to get a better job, or decides to work two or three jobs in order to save more of his hard-earned dollars to buy a better house, live in a better neighborhood, or put better clothes on his children's backs, that some government official isn't going to show up on his doorstep and say, "Thank you, now you can leave," because he has more than the next person and it isn't *fair*. I *hope* that one day he doesn't decide to put away his ambition, his drive, his determination or his God-given gifts, because they do him no good. I *hope* that he never feels that a solid work ethic is of no use and no value, and that his time would be better spent getting into that food line or healthcare line or clothing line earlier, because while he was wasting time following ambition, everyone else got first pickings, then came to his house and took their *fair* share of whatever he made for himself. Hope? Let's look at the Webster's Dictionary definition of Hope . . .

HOPE
1. a feeling that what is wanted will happen; desire accompanied by expectation. **2.** the thing that one has a hope for. **3.** a reason for hope. **4.** a person or thing on which a person may base some hope. **5.** trust; reliance.

Okay, so now that we have established that Hope is not a system of government, but is instead a feeling or an emotion or the subject thereof, let us objectively look at what is really needed in this country. *Change* was another predominant theme in this election year and has been often throughout history. The question is, *change* to what? Is anyone hoping for change for the worse? Right. What we need in this country are changes for the better. Yet, change for the better is something about which our two-party system can never agree. Why? For the most part, it's a matter of political power and expediency. Have you noticed how little our president or our Congress ever get done for *We The People*. Perhaps I missed something, but I'm pretty sure that we put them in office to serve us. Yet, all I recall hearing from our elected government over the course of the last year is the endangered Federal Budget. What about the budgets of *We The People?* If you people on Capitol Hill can't balance your finances, STOP SPENDING OUR MONEY! There, solved that problem.

What we need to agree about more than anything else in this country is the philosophy of government. That's really what our Constitution is all about. That's what our Founding Fathers and every great leader we've had since were about. Any student of history will tell you that a society's philosophy was the key to their advancement, decline, extinction or absence from history altogether, because they were a *never was.* The United States of America was founded on two primary philosophies that work hand in hand. We are a democratic Republic and we function under a capitalistic economy. On the former, that means we elect a representative government. We are not a true democracy, which proved a failure in ancient Greece. Simply put, you can never get the *mob* to agree long enough to get anything productive done in a time of crisis or other-wise. Concerning capitalism, this is the exact opposite of socialism and communism. Since both the latter forms of government have produced failure upon failure throughout history, I guess that would mean capitalism is the opposite of failure, right? Darn right it is.

Now, does that mean that there should be no restraints to curb capitalistic tendencies towards greed and excess? Of course not, but tread lightly. Anything more than the most judicious, careful and delicate interference with capitalism will not result in the *redistribution of wealth,* but a weakening of the middle and lower classes. Almost always, the hindrance of capitalism results in the opposite of intended consequences. Why? You have to understand that the barons of capitalist enterprise, business and investment are so well-insulated from economic strife that they hardly feel the pinch. Instead, over-burdening business only has the effect of those burdens being passed down to the rest of us. Once we become overloaded, that's when you see what is happening with the economy today, and what has happened off and on throughout history. Are the rich worried about unemployment, maintaining shelter, buying food or getting health care? NO. They have stashed away enough money to weather a thousand periods of biblically proportioned *lean*. When times of plenty come again, they'll pull their money out of their vaults, reinvest and society will renew its growth and expansion as it has throughout this country's history.

I can hear it now, *You're giving all the reasons why spreading the wealth is a good thing!* Are they right though? No, they are precisely missing the point. So, if you are among the socialist-propaganda guzzling crowd, please go back to your University and ask for a refund. THEY BAMBOOZLED YOU!

Look at it this way; extremes of almost any sort are unhealthy. The reality about socialism is that any bit of it is, by definition, extreme. What we need to have in this country is a dialogue about how to make a more productive, robust and lasting capitalistic society. I'll be the first to agree that the rich are getting richer and that the poor are getting poorer, and that Middle America is fast sliding into the category of poverty. Warning to the Rich! If we lose the middle-class in this country, then we are going to be looking at real change all right. It will be change at the end of a gun. Sound extreme? Check your history? Opulent societies throughout history who have neglected to support the middle-class were ultimately overthrown, hanged and had all their wealth and riches redistributed to the masses. Now, nobody in their right mind in this country wants to see that happen, yet I fear we may be headed in that direction. Inching our way into socialism will only speed that process up, trust me. Why? Because never in history has a socialist program resulted in the growth and expansion of an economy. Without expansion and growth our children won't have an abundance of jobs to choose from, if any. Without jobs our children won't earn a living. Need I go on?

Folks, this is some serious stuff. We have been sliding with ever-increasing speed towards socialism since FDR's *New Deal* was implemented in 1933. It was supposed to pull America out of the Great Depression, but it didn't. Find a historian that tells you different and call them a L-I-A-R, because that is exactly what they are. Never in the course of human history has government ever bailed a society out of economic dire straits. Sure, plenty of governments of all types, democratic or despotic have protected a country from being conquered in military conquest, but that is about it. Likewise, a government can organize a society to accomplish a great many public works that can expedite economic growth and development, but be careful. A government's ability to engage in public projects comes at the expense of the people, and thus is limited by the success of the people. Get it? Let me say it a different way. If there are no tax dollars in the coffer, as is the case today, then it is time to get off the people's backs and think about putting off any grand government plans until things get back on track.

So what happened? Why did America feel like it needed a *New Deal?* Well, we were in a Depression for one. I don't know about you, but whenever I've been depressed, I usually wasn't thinking too clear. The Great Depression was set in motion as a result of a concurrence of events beginning with the stock market crash on Black Tuesday, October 29, 1929. The stock market had surged tremendously in the years prior, as had the use of credit and an excess of government spending. Sound familiar? Everything didn't come crashing to a halt on one day either. The American economy didn't bottom out until 1933, up to which point there had been multiple false signs of economy recovery. So what got our country into this boat in the first place? It's never just one thing. A collapse of that monumental proportion is a result of multiple failures. Heading up the list, given my research on the subject, was Investment Speculation in the stock market. Sounds a lot like real estate speculation doesn't it? Another catalyst was a tremendous and unprecedented drought in the Midwest, which severely damaged crop production. Again, sound familiar given the present drought conditions in the Midwest? You didn't know about that? Look it up and you will find that meteorologists believe we are in the exact same weather cycle as we experienced in the early 1930s. Some other causes for the Depression are reported to have included a rising national debt, out of control inflation followed by dramatic deflation, punishing foreign import tariffs, bank runs, bank failures, money hoarding, frozen credit, lack of capital liquidity . . . the list goes on. It was ultimately a chain reaction where one crisis caught fire to another. Who was to blame? That's a debate for the ages, raged by every side of the philosophical equation from Marxists to capitalists and all the iterations thereof. FDR and his administration blamed greedy corporations, although that seems politically expedient to me.

At the core of the *"What failed?"* debate, is the question between macro and micro-economics. Okay, bear with me for a second . . . Macroeconomics is the philosophy that things like credit availability and capital liquidity, or how much cash is made available to the financial system for lending, drive the economy. This is the prevailing wisdom of those who presently preside over our financial system, and thus gave us the $700 billion-dollar bailout plan. Lord help me! Microeconomics is the philosophy that people like you and me actually drive the economy as we decide what to buy, what not to buy, invest or not to invest, etc. Guess where I fall?

Now before all you economic geniuses start getting up in arms, I am not pretending to be an expert on economics. Come by my house in Toledo and you will quickly find the answer to that question. However, what I am saying is that it doesn't take a genius to understand what's wrong with our economy right now. It's all about common sense. Any of you recall your grandparents, or perhaps great-grandparents pestering you about how you need to save, save, save? Guess why, because they saw firsthand that in hard economic times the difference between shelter and no shelter and food or starvation was money in the bank—or perhaps in the mattress. Sure, financial experts are going to say I'm irresponsible, that hiding money in the mattress or a hole in the backyard will only make the situation worse. But of course they're going to say that. They are tied into the system that is hosing you and me down.

So, you're asking yourself, *"Just who is to blame?"* Are you sure you want to know? Okay, here you go . . .

YOU ARE.

That's right. If you have more debt than you can shake a stick at, if you paid top dollar for a house that doesn't have a big enough garage or decent backyard, if you put all your savings into a 401-K and didn't watch it, or if you can't live without the latest new electronic gadget at Buy Me Here, Buy Me Now USA Superstore, then you have only yourself to blame. I'm not sorry to say it, but I am sorry for anyone who has to learn a hard lesson right now. We can empathize with one another through these hard times, but that won't put us on the right path—that is, the *right road*.

So let's talk about how we get out of this mess. It ain't gonna happen by some *Spreading The Wealth* program. No, talking about *Hope* ain't gonna do it either, although we'll need to cling to hope to endure what is needed. Are you ready for it? Are you sure you want to know? Okay, here goes it . . .

HARD WORK.

I can hear the laughter and the chants now from the Left, *Joe the Idiot, Joe the Idiot* . . . Well Mr. and Mrs. Collegiate Elite, if you are still in a trade that makes use of that fancy degree you have penned on the wall by this time next year, then congratulations. You are among the ultra-rich for whom this crisis will not really matter. However, if you are not, I hope you are right and I am wrong.

In the event I am right, let's talk about what sort of Hard Work it will take to get on that *right road*. First thing you're going to have to do is whittle down your debt. Don't be among the last in the country to do so or you will be sorry, trust me. If you don't have the income, then cut back on expenses. If you have already done that, then get credit relief help. There are plenty of organizations that will help you plan and implement your own bailout. However, the most important thing you can do is to start saving money, RIGHT NOW! You don't need to do anything fancy unless you have enough money to hire an accountant who can help you make sound investment decisions. However, if you are in my boat, then you just need to get down to your local FDIC-insured bank and open a simple interest-bearing savings account. Start putting as many bucks as you can every day, week and month into that account.

Okay, now that we have taken care of the immediate need, the long-term plan is more difficult. It involves dialing back government interference in our lives. What's worse, is that if (or when) the economy slips more, the government will try to step in and stop it, and by doing so, will only make it worse. Need proof? Okay, have you seen any of the $700 billion-dollar bail out? That's what I thought. We need to wake up and smell the coffee—whoops, I forgot coffee is too expensive anymore. Roses? Nope, unless you grow them yourself. Okay, just wake up! Contact your elected officials to oppose any bill that equates to more ridiculous bailouts. If you are too busy working to follow these things, good for you. Just read the final chapter of this book and I will have a solution for you.

We have only just begun, so let's start to talk about the real Hard Work that will be needed to survive the hard times that are coming. First, keep working and do the best job you can for your employer. If you are unfortunate enough to become a casualty of a corporate layoff or merger or failure, or already have, then get a job, whatever job you can as fast as you can. Don't be too selective or too proud. Better job opportunities will and always do come to those with a great work ethic. That doesn't mean you won't have to tighten your belt or do work you don't like for a while, but at least you and your family will keep your house and will always have food on the table to eat. In hard times, you shouldn't complain when at the very least you have that. If you are already complaining, then stop. Whiners never prosper, they just get trampled on by the doers.

Listen, I guarantee you that if things get worse in this country, soon Obama or another politician from either political party will start talking about the New Deal for the twenty-first century. Read my lips, WE DON'T NEED IT AND WE DON'T WANT IT.

Seriously people, this the last thing we need. Our American Dream hasn't recovered from the first deal. Another such *deal* may doom us. Just remember that any kind of government bailout amounts to more socialism. Anyone still questioning what socialism will do to our economy and our American Dream? If you are saying yes, go back and reread this entire book. Still not convinced? I guess that means you are working for the other side and you are reading this book to research the stratagem of your enemy.

After accepting personal responsibility and resigning oneself to hard work, there yet remains more we must do. What I'm about to suggest is even harder than the first two, because in hard times it is counterintuitive to basic human emotion. Okay, are you ready? Here goes it . . .

WE MUST TAKE CARE OF EACH OTHER.

Yes, it is really that simple. You don't need to go far and wide to search for those in need either. When economies tumble, someone in almost every neighborhood in the country will need your helping hand. Perhaps folks in The Hamptons won't need it, but just about everywhere else will. Reach out to your neighbors and don't let them lose their homes. Don't let your brother or sister starve or go without healthcare. Give them a lift to work if they can't afford money for gas. Help them find a job if they're struggling. Most important, if you are among the blessed in this country that do have great wealth, or better than average wealth and you can stand to *share* some of it, or a lot, THEN DO SO! Give someone a job, even if there is not enough work to go around. Don't lay someone off if you can afford to avoid it, and I don't mean in the sense of sustaining those record profits you have been gleaning these last five to six years. Pay your employees' medical bill if they become stricken with illness or disease. I guarantee you they will come back to work when able and give you twice the output and be twice as loyal. It will feel good. Giving always feels good. The more you have to give the more you get to feel good. So how blessed are you then?

Listen, if you are one of these corporate gluttons or a mid-to-large-size business owner sitting down reading this and find yourself saying, *What the heck is this guy talking about?* WAKE UP! If you can afford to spend a little of that money in your coffer to keep your employees working, fed and healthy, then don't hesitate. Your money will come back to you. Even if you're a pessimist and you think that no one is really going to take this advice, then you have to at least admit that a little Christian spirit will pay off in the long run. If you have never given much in your life, besides an honest wage for an honest day's pay—which is good, don't misunderstand me—then you are missing out on something HUGE. I have always gotten back three times what I have put in. I don't expect it, that's just what happens. God rewards those who reward themselves.

Here's the deal, and if you have been a successful business-person then you already know that we all must lead by example. Become a part of the story that is the solution and not an example of the problem upon which historians will one day reflect. If we stand together and tell government, "Back off, we've got this covered," imagine just how bright the future will be. Naturally, you don't think that sitting in your office waiting for this thing to blow over is going to secure your piece of the American Dream, do you? No, you don't. You have already demonstrated an understanding that taking the initiative and working hard breeds success in this country. You have seen what fruits your labors have brought you. You have lived the reality of the American Dream.

If you do not personally do something about the state of this country and get involved, I guarantee you will come to regret it. You will become a sad casualty among many, and miss out on your opportunity to stand out as a shining example among the few. If you take up the banner with me, then I will do everything in my power to make you famous. I will herald your business as a model for capitalism in our country, the kind of business that has a conscience and should be supported by every red-blooded American citizen that has a dime to spend towards your goods and services.

If you are yawning right now, then don't bother engaging me and wasting my time or the many that will stand beside me. We are looking for winners, not sluggards who foolishly believe Uncle Sam is going to make your bed for you every night. In this country we stand for exceptionalism, not mediocrity. We would have never driven past the Mississippi over the Rockies and to the Pacific Coast were it not for our winning spirit. We wait for no one. We drive ahead where no one else dare go and no one else has the courage to follow. We are not the Canadians. We are not the French. We are not Mexico, nor are we the United Nations. We are the United States of America and we lead that the rest of the world may follow!

10

Taking Sides

When I found out that shortly after the presidential debate my supposedly confidential state records had been accessed and shared illegally by those in the employ of the State of Ohio, I was devastated. I was scared, and I mean really scared. The media and other groups slandering me on airwaves, print and on the Internet was bad enough. But to find out that the information they had on me was likely provided to them by officials within the Ohio State Government? WOW! Have you ever had something of significance stolen before, like a radio out of your car, or worse, something out of your house? Remember that naked feeling, the sense that you're being watched, that a part of your privacy had been stripped from you? Now multiply that feeling times one hundred, no one thousand. These people were not just out to discredit me, they were out to do me personal harm. I just kept asking myself, *Why? They don't even know me. All I asked was a simple question and now they're going through my personal records? Are you kidding me?*

As one might imagine, the mercury in my stress-o-meter shot right out the top. Normally I can handle the stress of bad tidings, even personal threats. Yet, the effect on my mom, my dad and my son Joey really put me on edge. I asked myself just how large a target had I become? Was it going to get worse? Were our lives going to be in danger? Just think about that for a second. I started to summarize in my mind all the media coverage I had received, all the commentaries, all the questions, the support mail and the hate mail. Everyone was painting me as some kind of monumental figure, a portrait of the anti-Obama candidate. Did they somehow forget that I was just a plumber? I wasn't running for anything. I didn't want to run for anything, although that rumor got started too.

In the early days of this revelation, I prayed long, I prayed hard and I prayed often, desperately seeking the Lord's counsel. I had just become a full-time father to my son again. What if some whacko were to show up at my house wanting more than an interview? I strongly contemplated taking the whole family into hiding somewhere for another week or so until the election was over. When I considered the possibility that McCain might win, I wondered if there was anywhere in America we could feel safe again. This led me to the obvious conclusion that I would do no more interviews for anyone.

In spite of being overtaken by a severe and numbing fear, as often happens when you put yourself at the Lord's mercy you begin to see things beyond mortal reckoning. I started to realize that if I disappeared, I was giving these vermin exactly what they wanted. They weren't just seeking my personal financial and emotional collapse, it was my voice they wanted to silence. I was to know my place and shut my mouth. It was a clear message too. *If you don't shut up, it's only going to get worse.*

Pretty soon my fear subsided in place of anger and then frustration. Who do these people think they are? Are they not the *threat from within* our great presidents and Founding Fathers had so fervently tried to warn us about? These are the people who spit on our Constitution and desecrate our flag. Why? For nothing more than the sake of their party, their team, they would trample upon all that we hold dear in this country, for which we spilt blood and from which these ingrates have reaped so much.

Almost immediately after the debate, I was contacted by a 527 organization to do an ad. It was somewhat of a creepy experience. They had a script prepared and all the pieces in position to play my ad in each of the key swing states repeatedly until Election Day. I was told that if I really wanted to do some good and have an impact on this election, this ad was the best way. It was also suggested that when the dust settled and McCain had won, I would be owed and I would be rewarded. Naturally, they gave no specifics beyond a wink-wink and a nod-nod. *Scratch our back, Joe, and we'll set you up for life.* I flatly turned it down. It's not that I disagreed with the words in the script, because it was nothing more than I had already been saying on various news networks. It was the nature of these 527's and their ads on the air. They are like political attack pit bulls. I believe in Free Speech and everyone's right to engage in it, but this deal just felt wrong to me. It felt like a cheap shot on Obama and exploitive. However, they did say one thing that has stuck with me, and continues to echo today. They said, "Joe their attacks have only begun. You belong with us. We will watch your back. Don't sit out there in the open and let them take potshots at you. They're probably digging through all your records right now, trying to find some dirt they can bury you with . . ."

Clearly there are both pawns and captains at work in this game, and from both sides. I can imagine the Republican machine has done some pretty crappy things to their rivals as well, but a private citizen?

I have made a conscious decision to go after those who wronged me, and my pursuit for justice has only just begun. They cannot succeed with their attempts to silence me. I cannot forget the immortal words of Edmund Burke. I will not be that *man in America who does nothing.* I will not sit idly by and watch all the hope and promise of this great nation slide into the cesspool of government corruption. I realized I had to fight for the sake of Joey and all that I love and hold dear. I just kept thinking, *What if it is my generation that Reagan spoke of? Could it have come so soon?* These people need to be found-out and exposed. They need to be removed from their positions of access to sensitive information. Those who used them, supported them or encouraged them to misuse and abuse their position to harm me, also need to be exposed and need to pay a price for their ill deeds. I don't care how high it goes and who all is involved, I won't rest until justice is served and other folks can be assured that their Constitutional Right to challenge their elected officials will not be infringed upon by the same system of government that is supposed to represent and protect them.

Reagan was right, and that generation that lets slip our freedoms into the archives of tragic history could well be ours. We have a civic duty and moral obligation in this country to challenge our elected officials. The day we do not, we may as well burn the Constitution and line up at the Socialist Food Mart, because that is where they, the government will take us.

I mentioned it before, but the greatest irony of this invasion of my privacy is that it had the exact opposite effect from what they had hoped. I started engaging the media more, making my voice heard at every turn. Instead of avoiding interviews and reporters, I began inviting them in. "Sure I'll talk to you," I would say. Some of the media didn't quite understand it at first, but they were plenty happy to get my story.

What was my goal? Well it wasn't necessarily to spirit McCain to victory. Clearly, nothing could have made that scenario happen. My message was simple. I am an American citizen and therefore I have a right to ask my elected officials tough questions, much less a simple one. I told everyone who would listen that I was afraid for America, and I meant it. If you must ask why, then you have not been paying attention.

Did Obama unfairly bear the blame and my ire for the things that happened to me? If he did, I don't think he is any worse for the wear. I have harbored no ill feelings for him, nor do I today. As I have stated repeatedly, Obama was gracious, respectful and polite that day I spoke with him. Although it appears that the ultra-liberal wing of his party was behind most of the slanderous attacks that came my way, I have no reason to believe he was behind it. He didn't seem to have a problem addressing a direct question from a private citizen. You've seen the tape, haven't you?

Here remains the sticky question; considering all the absurd and depraved filth that has been thrown at me and the sources from which it all comes, why is Obama their guy? Why on the day following his victory did all our enemies throughout the world leap at their chance to congratulate him? Would they have done the same for McCain? I guess we will never know.

People, I'm scared to death about what tomorrow may bring for America. I am one of those people who just can't understand why someone like Ahmadinejad, a man who openly supports "Death to America," can step onto our soil and we don't automatically throw his butt in a box and ship him down to Guantanamo. If you think he should be able to step up to the United Nations podium in New York City and rail against the country that has graciously given him a stage, then are you really interested in protecting our freedoms?

This is why I cannot and will not be silenced. I asked myself what kind of message I would be sending to regular Middle America if I did disappear. In nearly two weeks after that fateful debate, I had received hundreds of letters from regular folks like you. Some of you just wanted to share your story with me. Some of you encouraged, while others strongly urged me to continue the fight. I could hardly believe the outpouring of support from absolute strangers. You all didn't know me. All you really knew about me before reading this book was from a collection of interviews, but I guess you all saw something that hit close to home. For that reason, I realized I not only had a duty to myself to continue on, but I had a civic duty to all of you. What would you have thought of me if I hadn't? What would you do if ever given the chance to question an elected official, knowing what had happened to me?

After much prayer and counseling with family and friends, I at last came to the conclusion that I needed to stand up for Middle America and announce my vote, or my endorsement as it was. This should have come as no surprise to anyone. In fact, many of you and many in the media couldn't understand why a *Joe The Plumber* bus tour was on the road for the McCain campaign and yet I wasn't on it.

The weekend before I made my decision to announce my choice for president, I distinctly remember watching a CNN misreport that I was indeed "now on tour with John McCain." Wow, maybe I could just stay at home and watch my tour unfold like the rest of America. Today, as I reflect upon the journey that was yet to come, I often wonder if I shouldn't have done just that. Did I really make a difference? Did anyone benefit from my outspoken voice? You all will have to be the judge of that. I only know that you can trust the media for answers no more than you can trust politicians. I also know that had I not made my decision, I would not have learned so much about myself, as well as what truly ails our country.

11

The Regular Joes

The ultimate reason *why* I had leaned towards the Republican ticket all along and eventually determined that I needed to support McCain is both simple and complex. I know, I'm not supposed to be the *complex* kind of guy, but these are the days for simple solutions, not simple-mindedness. The one thing I will always respect about McCain is his dedicated service to our country. He bled for us during his days in that Vietnam prison. Despite having met him in person, I don't know the man's soul any better than you, but I can assure you that enduring years of torture will change a man. A part of your life will be gone, and though you may turn that experience to good, the impact of so much evil will have lingering effects.

A personal note to Senator McCain . . .
Sir, if ever you come to read this book, then understand that despite anything about which we may disagree, I honor your service.

Aside from McCain's service and sacrifice in the military, which again I hold in the highest esteem, my outspoken support for him and my eventual vote were not based upon what I hoped he would do for me as president. With blunt honesty, I did not want him for the Republican ticket. I do not agree with a great many of his policies, nor do I care for aspects of his voting record. Two primary examples of his proposed policies that bothered me were his plan for a $5000 health-care credit to every family and his support for the financial system bailout. These policies are socialist in nature and frankly little better than what Obama has proposed.

So why support McCain? He was the last hope for some semblance of conservative capitalism in this country for at least the next four years. Confused? Don't be. It is a simple fact of modern-day party politics. If one party controls Congress and another the White House, as we had during the Clinton years, then government doesn't get much of anything done and America can take care of getting to business for America. However, when you have both parties controlling the Executive and Legislative Branches of government, as you had with Bush in his first term and will now have with Obama during his, LOOK OUT! Yes, it may strike you as odd that I was not so crazy about my supposed party having control of everything either. Like I told you, I am for limited government, period. McCain was a vote for limited government and someone who might put another strict constructionist judge on the Supreme Court. God knows what will happen now. Fact is, that if McCain ever got into office, my hope and prayer was that he would accomplish nothing and would see to it that the likes of Speaker Pelosi and Senate Majority Leader Harry Reid didn't get anything done either. My greatest fear was that either of these naturally two opposing sides might reach across the aisle to each other to pass new legislation. Sorry, but I'm a pretty straightforward guy and I don't believe in the power of government to solve our problems. *They* the government only make things worse.

Committed to my new mission, I reached out to my local Republican Party headquarters and asked them to get a message to McCain that I wanted to come out and support him. They were ecstatic as one might imagine. Somehow I was not.

It wasn't long before I received a response from McCain's campaign officials, who advised me to sit tight and wait for them to come up with a strategy. I wasn't really sure what they meant by that. I figured they would just come pick me up and we'd hightail it out to wherever McCain or Palin were so we could meet up and get to it. I guess somehow it was more complicated than that.

Over the course of the next two days, I must have gotten a dozen or more mixed messages from the McCain camp. They couldn't figure out what they were going to do with me and I started to reflect on all I had heard on the news about his dysfunctional campaign team. I mean, couldn't they just put me on my tour bus, wherever it was in the country? It was the *Joe The Plumber* bus tour was it not?

Eventually we did arrange for me to join a local Ohio bus tour of *Regular Joes* scheduled for Tuesday, just a short week from the election. I was to tag along with a collection of small-business owners, including Mary the Flag Lady, Mike the Painter, Cathy the Pool Supply Lady, Lucy the Florist, and Linda the Fitness Trainer. My hat's off to each of them. They were all great people, fun to be with and are true examples of the American Dream. I may have been the headliner of the event, but these folks are the real deal. It is they, and so many others like them, who may suffer from an overburdensome and ultimately destructive White House tax initiative.

It was a cold and windy morning when I arrived at the local campaign office to meet up with the bus and these small-business heroes. Republican Party staff ushered me up to the third floor of the building where I was welcomed by a number of volunteers and campaign coordinators. The excitement was humbling. They all greeted me with applause and words of encouragement, then proceeded to ask for autographs and pose with me for pictures. It was very uncomfortable for me, although I really appreciated the expression of support. I started to understand how important my voice had been to people, and there were more of you than I could have imagined.

It wasn't long before former Congressman Rob Portman, who would be joining us, arrived and came over to introduce himself. I was happy to meet him and found him to be a regular guy. I thought everyone in the office should have been paying far greater attention to him than they were to me. After all, I had never served a public post, aside from my term of service in the Air Force.

After Rob showed up, it was time to hit the road, although that was easier said than done. I just don't know how to say no to folks who politely engage me. I still feel bad about anyone in that office that didn't a get a picture with me, my autograph or a moment to speak with me. It's not that I'm that important, because I'm most certainly not. I just like to give people the same level of generosity they show me.

Once they were able to drag me away and load me onto the bus, I got a chance to meet the small-business owners that were the true stars of the day. I found each of their stories fascinating and uniquely American. God bless them for their hard work and for having the courage to go out and grab their piece of the American Dream. Not a one of them didn't understand the values I speak of in this book; the hard work, a need for limited government, appreciation for our Founding Fathers, and a Faith in God and His blessings, for without them, no Dream would be possible.

Our first stop on the tour was going to be at Mary The Flag Lady's store in Columbus. As the bus drove around to the parking lot, we spotted several protesters picketing outside, though not enough to make a baker's dozen. Let me repeat that—protesters picketing me, Joe The Plumber, as if I was running for office. A part of me wanted to laugh, and then as I thought about it, I was disappointed. First of all, why does anyone need to protest anything about an election? Let the candidates speak to their constituents and then let your vote be the ultimate protest. Protesting a candidate's appearance to speak, much less a mere supporter for a candidate is just plain asinine. What does that accomplish, except to infringe upon one side's right to Free Speech? I guess that's it then, isn't it. As I said, it was disappointing.

As we exited the bus, I was surprised to see that police had cordoned the place off to keep the protestors from interfering with our procession to the Flag Lady's store. That was another disappointment, realizing that Americans were footing the bill to pay those officers not to fight crime and track down criminals, but to keep the peace for a campaign stump. Boy, don't get me started . . .

Amidst some mean-spirited and downright nasty shouts from the protestors, we entered Mary's store. Wow, what a great place! I love flags, especially patriotic and historic flags of our country's past. She had all that and more. Her store was great, and I highly recommend you make a point to go there if you are ever in Columbus, Ohio.

When we entered the main area of her store, I was welcomed by a massive throng that probably broke a great many fire codes. There was hardly a square inch between them, and their eruption of cheers and applause was overwhelming. I became immediately self-conscious. If you haven't figured it out yet, I really cherished my anonymity before this ordeal began. Yet, the swell of positive energy I felt in that room was like nothing I had experienced to that point. It was invigorating and uplifting, but also scary. Who was I to receive such fanfare?

Amidst a flurry of photograph flashes, handshakes and pats on the back, Rob led me and the rest of the real celebrity small-business owners, including Mary over to a podium which had been setup before a small group of news people with cameras. I really didn't know what all had been announced or coordinated for this tour, so I was curious about where this event might be broadcasted. It made me nervous, because I knew I would be expected to offer some words, and I am not by any stretch an accomplished speaker. I can do Q&A with a reporter or commentator no problem, but make a speech? Uh, yeah—no.

After the chants of "Joe, Joe, Joe . . ." died down, Rob stepped forward and spoke. He had prepared notes and talked about how great McCain was for small business and so on. Nothing against Rob, but it was typical political speak, citing statistics, policy differences with Obama and what it all means to the small-business owner.

A good friend of mine, who was on this journey with me every step of the way, later told me that no one paid much mind to it. All the anticipation was about me, and what I would say. I'll take his word for it, because all I could think of during that moment was what I was going to say. One might think that McCain's people would have given me a script to memorize, but they didn't, and I would in no wise have accepted one anyhow. Nope, all I had were my words and my wits, which don't always come out as clear as I would like.

Rob finally came to the point where he introduced each of the small-business owners who had gathered, with special thanks to Mary, and then introduced me. Again, the cheers and applause erupted, and I really didn't like it. It's not that I didn't appreciate the support, because I did. I just thought that I was a small figure amongst giant-folk who were really struggling to make their small businesses thrive.

I stepped forward in Rob's place and must have looked beet-red, particularly with my large-sized cranium. I have been in tough situations in my life, but none of them in any way prepared me for stage fright. When their applause subsided, for the first time in the election I put forth my voice for a specific candidate and call to action. I can't remember verbatim all that I said, and I know it didn't come out with the eloquence I would have liked. In fact, I remember asking those gathered to forgive my sluggish tongue, explaining to them that I wasn't accustomed to speaking. To that, they graciously began applauding and giving me further encouragement.

"You're doing great Joe," they said.

The main points of my brief and awkward speech were what I had been saying all along, which was for folks to get informed about the issues and get involved in the political process. I might have said something to the effect of "That's why I'm voting for a real American, John McCain," but that was about it. If it sounded short and choppy, you have to understand I was about as uncomfortable as one can get. Consider how relaxed you would be standing out in front of the cameras to share your vote with all of America. Add on top of that all the awful things the media and political-smear machines were doing to me at the time. Boy, the pressure was really on.

I later heard a variety of media reports, along with some grumblings within McCain's camp, that they didn't care for my *real American* label. To that I say, too bad if you don't like it. That's how I feel. I don't believe that only because you are born in this country or become legally naturalized that it gives you the right to call yourself an American. I don't mean this in the legal sense. That point is made clear in the Constitution. What I mean, is that if you don't love this country with all your heart, the values and principles for which it stands, and forsake love of any other nation, then you are not really an American in my book. I share that point of view with T.R., and I'm pretty proud to be in his great company with this sentiment.

Shortly after I finished speaking, the questions rang out from the press. I was worried they would ask me to describe the specific McCain policies I supported over Obama. Uh, let's see, "I hope he succeeds in grid-locking government until we can get a better candidate in there." Yeah, I'm sure that would have gone over well. It's hardly the kind of awe-inspiring message that would have encouraged folks to move away from Obama or those straddling the fence to lean towards McCain.

However, instead of asking me hard-hitting questions, which you want the press to do, they threw me softballs. It was more or less the same kinds of questions that I had been answering for the last two weeks. They did ask me, "Why now?" That was easy to answer, because why not? Everyone I listened to agreed that this was the most important election in our lifetime, so why should I sit the bench and leave it up to all the usual suspects to fumble over themselves trying to get *their guy* elected?

After a few questions, I happily surrendered the stage to Mary. It was her store after all. She should have been doing all the talking, and she had a lot to say. I loved it. Her story is what makes this country so great. It's an American story.

Mike the Painter also had a great story to share. He started his business from scratch, no business plan, no money, and no fear! He and his wife made it work. I felt like jumping up and down shouting YEAH! That's the way to get it done in this country.

After a couple of speeches, among which mine was the least insightful, we were running late and about to disengage when suddenly a man called out for me from the back of the crowd, "Joe! Joe The Plumber!"

It was a strange and awkward moment, and akin to that day I questioned Obama. All who were gathered went silent and parted the way so that this man and I could look each other eye-to-eye. He was an elderly gentleman, but clearly strong of mind and spirit as he spoke. He explained that he was Jewish and had come up all the way from Florida to meet me, and to see if I would support his viewpoint that "A vote for Obama will be a vote for the death of Israel."

Since that incident, some have suggested that this was some sort of mudslinging setup, planned by the McCain campaign. Absolutely not. It was as real as real can get. I shared a special moment with this man and I expressed my support for his fear. I told the truth about my own fear. If you are a Christian and believe in the words of the Bible, then protection of Israel is essential to our own salvation. If you don't believe in the religious aspect of this, you have to agree that it would be an absolute crime of the highest moral failure to allow Israel's enemies to consume her, as they well want to do. Who else do we have in that region that supports America and shares our ideals, Iran?

We made a couple more stops at The Dublin Pub in Dayton, Ohio, great place, great people, great food; then at Cathy the Pool Supply Lady's business, called S&S Pools in Middletown, Ohio. At each stop I was able to improve upon my speechmaking skills, but didn't nearly become comfortable with the outward expressions of support from the folks. I literally needed to grow two other sets of hands in order to shake all those that were cast in my direction. I also had to learn how to sign my name a lot faster in order to keep up with demand. It was just plain nuts! Cheers, pictures, hugs, stories, you name it and it came my way that day. It was impossible to keep up and stay on schedule. At the Dublin Pub, I went out back just to get a breather while the rest of our tour group sat and ate. Even by the garbage cans people kept coming up to me for autographs and pictures. Unreal! God bless them all. I hope I didn't let them down then or have since.

During the press conference at S&S Pools my earlier encounter with the Jewish man hit the news. I was fairly surprised it took that long. I have to tell you that being a newsmaker is a strange and surreal experience. One moment you're having a discussion face-to-face with someone and the next thing you know, everyone on the airwaves is talking about it. What's fascinating is how just moments after the words leave your mouth nearly half of all reports either completely misquote you or omit key elements, which is why you hear so many in the media spotlight frequently say, "That was taken out of context." What's more amusing, is to watch political professionals try to control, or spin the news. So while I was preparing to address another crowd of press and regular folks at S&S Pools, the campaign organizers on the tour watching the rash of network news reports on the bus TV were burning up their cell phones and blackberries with McCain headquarters, trying to figure out how I needed to respond.

Now I don't aim to disappoint, but I wasn't about to back down from agreeing with that man's sentiment about Israel. I spoke from my heart to his and that's all there is to it. Must I lie for the sake of political correctness? I can't think of a lesser reason for which to lie.

I had received a call from a Fox News producer for Shepherd Smith's show earlier in the day before the incident, asking me if I would call in for an interview. I had agreed, but now everyone was freaking out about what Shep Smith might say or ask me, or perhaps they were afraid of what more I might say. But it's Fox, right? Weren't they the safe network for McCain?

Someone from the McCain headquarters called the bus and asked to speak with me before the interview. He had prepared some talking points for me to relate to Shep. Imagine that, talking points. I always hated the sound of that. He asked me if I had heard of Rashid Khalidi. I told him I had, but was not fully informed. He proceeded to explain to me that this man was a Palestinian terrorist with whom Obama had a personal relationship, and that the L.A. Times was refusing to release footage of a dedication dinner for him that Obama had emceed. That all sounded interesting and concerning, but I had not personally educated myself on the facts of these reports. I wasn't about to take some campaign person's word and regurgitate it to Fox. Would you have? If you answered yes, go back and reread this entire book. You have much to learn about what is wrong with this country today and what we must do to bring it back to right.

As I got off the phone with McCain's HQ, I'll never forget the tension on the bus leading up to my interview with Shep. I admit that I was somewhat annoyed by it. I didn't care what Fox News or anyone else thought. I shared a moment with that Jewish man from Florida and I said what I believed. Should I now apologize? In order to justify my sentiments, was I to pad it with details, which for me weren't proven fact?

At the appointed time, I was called by Fox News and patched into Shepherd Smith. He sure did not sound happy. In fact, if I didn't know any better, I'd say he was disgusted. His tone and aggressive posture spoke a deep contempt for me, a presumed redneck hick, idiot-xenophobe from backwoods USA. Although I'm convinced Shep would argue that he is a professional and impartial reporter of the news, he had me fooled that day. As I had already stated, people cannot help but to insert their emotions and opinions into especially emotional and opinionated subjects. Shepherd proved this fact with every word, gesture and expression during that interview. He reported, you decide . . .

Regardless of the tone and bias of questions that came my way about Israel that day and many times thereafter, I have always had the same response; LOOK IT UP AND DECIDE FOR YOURSELF! When you do, you will either need to have your head examined or you will see that now President-elect Obama has closely associated with a shady list of characters who do not care for America, neither do they like Israel. Compound Obama's friendly relations with his desire to sit down with Ahmadinejad, whose stated main goal in life it to see the absolute destruction and desolation of the state of Israel, not to mention the United States, and you have to wonder if that old Jewish man wasn't just plain speaking the bold truth. I thought he was sincere, and I was there. I looked him in the eye and I saw and felt his concern. He wasn't some McCain plant. He was just another Middle American who had the courage to make his voice heard. Did you hear it? Would you tell that man he is not entitled to his honest to God opinion?

There were other stops, other words and repeated demonstrations of support for me, and that for which I think we all should stand as Americans. That idea of my civic duty that beat soundly in my heart, ceased to be an idea or mere feeling on that tour. To the hundreds of people I met that day, black, white, Christian, Jewish, Asian, German, Hispanic, young, old, male and female, YOU MADE IT REAL! You touched me, and the effects your kindness has not worn off even today. Sometimes you think you know you are on the *right road,* but seeing the signs along the way that prove the rightness of your direction is both heartening and empowering.

I also learned that day that you can never anticipate what you are going to find along the roads you choose. The greatest impression made upon me came from the Jewish man and his heartfelt desire to solicit my support for his honest fear. It is profound to me that I should be so important, but I discount it not. In spite of all that I experienced that day, this sentiment about Israel and our country's support for the birthplace of freedom is what stood out among the rest. I welcome and cherish it. It speaks to the heart of what this country is about and with whom we make our friendships. Have you not heard that the best way to judge a man is by the company he keeps? Let us pray that the fears of that man from Florida are unfounded and will remain unproven. Let us pray that my tongue was misguided and foolish. But let us be wise. Let us be vigilant. Let us not countenance evil to be reaped upon the good and the just.

If you find yourself questioning the importance of our connection with Israel, wander no farther than to what Thomas Jefferson once wrote, regarding the passing of his revered friend and fellow Founding Father, George Washington . . .

I felt on his death, with my countrymen, that 'verily a great man hath fallen this day in Israel.'

12

Meeting Sarah Palin

After freaking out everyone in the McCain camp with the "Death to Israel" flop, I did not receive immediate and energetic calls to get me back out on the trail the following day. Instead, there was deafening silence, and I wondered if they deemed me too great a liability to get anywhere near the true Republican ticket for this election.

The odd thing about my experience with the political campaign machine was just how fragmented and disorganized it seemed. One would think that I would have had a special contact assigned by McCain-HQ whose sole job was to direct and coordinate my movements. I kind of felt like, *Hello, I'm here, send me in coach!* Instead, I found myself juggling expectations from three different contacts that often didn't appear to be communicating with one another. More than once, I seriously considered disconnecting every electronic communication gadget I had and going into hiding until the election was over.

Around this time, the concept that I was somehow *cashing in* began circulating throughout the media. *Joe the country music star?* Uh, no. Did they think I was getting money from McCain or the Republican Party? That just didn't happen, was never offered nor would I have remotely considered accepting it. I have also heard that folks thought I was being paid for all those appearances on television and radio. Nope. Did I get a big advance for a book deal? Nope, I went with a small publisher to prove a point about supporting small business. The only thing I ever accepted was a paid lunch here and there, a hotel in New York for the weekend to visit Fox News for Huckabee, and a couple of airline tickets to get to appearances. Otherwise, I was unemployed, dead broke and using my last few dimes to drive myself out to McCain's and Palin's rallies.

Just when I thought my fifteen minutes (or fifteen days) of fame were up and my luck had changed for the better, the call did at last come. I was asked if I would be interested in joining Governor Sarah Palin on stage at Bowling Green State University for a rally. *Well, yes thank you I would. Forgive me for asking, but I pretty much came out to help the Republican ticket win this election, so what the heck is going on? Don't you all have a schedule for me for the rest of the week?* Although I was glad to be of some use, and yes, I was not afraid to be used for all the reasons I gave earlier, I was suspicious about what they were saying about me among the higher ranks of McCain's campaign team. Did they think I was a loose cannon? You don't want your candidate getting near one of them unless he or she is fireproof. Perhaps they figured that they had already established a *Joe The Plumber Campaign Tour*, so what was the point of having me on it. Maybe their problem was nothing more than they were indeed as dysfunctional as the media had portrayed them.

When the Wurzelbachers all awoke the day of the Palin rally, it was reminiscent of a Sunday preparation for church. That so happens to be the only day of the week I wear anything besides work shirts and work jeans, which is about all I have in my closet. I was, however, going to be formally meeting the potential next Vice President of the United States. In that case, I suppose a button-down shirt was in order.

Piling all the family into the car, with the exception of my mom who had to work, we quickly got on the road for a thirty-minute drive to the university. All the way there, aside from making sure I didn't get lost, my mind was crowded with thoughts of the unexpected. Did I really belong on stage with the likes of Governor Palin? Were they going to ask me to speak? Would the crowd accept me? If you remember any of the television footage of her rallies, you may recall the size of her crowds. Palin was packing them in, which meant I was going to be in front of thousands, not fifty-to-a-hundred. It made my stomach quiver. My typical comfort zone is in crawlspaces beneath houses, working in the mud. Need I say more?

When we arrived on campus, we had no escort and no detailed directions. They had only told us to show up. I didn't know who to ask for or where to park. I wasn't even sure if security at the school would know I was coming. In spite of all that, the first officer directing traffic we came upon quickly recognized me. He had a silly grin on his face as if to say, *Cool, I'm meeting Joe The Plumber.* Following protocol, and probably to be sure I wasn't a lookalike, he asked me to show him my ID, which I did. He then called the rest of the security folks over the radio to let them know I had arrived and directed us to VIP parking out near the basketball arena where the rally was to be held.

We parked, I said another prayer, already my fifth of the morning, and we walked out toward the arena's front entry. Soon as we turned the corner, I saw a thick line of Palin fans stretching far across campus. Almost immediately, they recognized me and erupted with a sudden burst of cheers and applause. I still wasn't used to it, and here were more people than I had seen all day long while I was out with the *Regular Joes* on the bus tour. I gave them all a brief and timid wave, which elicited an even greater response.

After being discovered, I wanted to get inside as quickly as possible. At the turnstiles we were greeted by security and ushered through. It didn't take long for the folks inside to also recognize me, and they started clapping and calling out my name. You would have thought I was a celebrity, which was a concept that I could not force through my thick skull.

My family and I were taken back to the locker rooms and briefed on the plan for the event, which evidently had not yet been fully conceived. I wondered if the Democrats equally struggled with planning and logistics. Considering the outcome of the election, I'd say probably not.

Later, my family was escorted to the VIP section of the stands to watch the event, while I was taken to a greenroom to await my chance to meet Governor Palin in person for the first time. It was an hour or more before Sarah and her entourage finally arrived. When they did, the door suddenly swung open and in came the Secret Service followed by Sarah and her husband Todd. She didn't see me at first, as I was blocked from view by the Secret Service, but when she did, she immediately turned to me and shook my hand.

"Hi Joe," she said, genuinely pleased to meet me, "you are a great American."

"*You* are a great American," I promptly told her.

I met Todd as well, who struck me as being a fish out of water, not unlike me. I think the two of us would have been happier at that moment out on the Chena River up in Alaska, fishing for salmon.

That was about all the time we had. Sarah was busily preparing for her speech and trying to keep pace with the schedule. We were going to have some time to chat later, so I didn't bother interrupting her with any questions or any challenges for that matter. She struck me as a focused and very capable politician, and I don't mean that in a negative sense, considering how I view most politicians. Since you're asking, no I wasn't overwhelmed by a great Washington-esk presence, yet I was impressed. Coming from someone who knows about hard work, I sensed in her a solid and committed work ethic. I can tell you right now that Palin earned every ounce of grain she got.

After a couple of warm-up acts, it was at last time for Governor Palin to head out on stage along with her husband Todd. The cheers and applause were deafening. It blew away anything that I had heard on my little road trip and I thought, *YES, this is it!* I was happy to see people more focused on someone besides me.

Sarah came up to the microphone and said a few rousing words, then the next thing I knew she was saying, "Joe The Plumber! C'mon out here!"

Well, here we go, I thought. *No turning back now.* I walked out into the arena and I was immediately hit with a blast from the roaring crowd. Oh man, I tell you what, nothing can prepare you for that! It was absolutely incredible. Aside from being so humbled by the moment and the energy throughout that area, I really could not believe that I was walking up on stage with Governor Palin. WOW!

From atop the stage I took in a panoramic view of the crowd. Whoa, was I ever relieved that we had agreed I would not speak. The place was jam-packed, on their feet and going nuts. Anything I could have said would only have ruined the moment.

When the crowd finally settled, Palin continued with her speech and I quickly found my son out in the VIP seats. He stood tall and proud so that I could pick him out. We locked eyes and I captured an indelible image of his giant smile and a son's pride in his father on his face. When I am old and seeing the last of my days, I will remember that moment and feel it like it was yesterday. It was all I could do not to breakdown right there on stage. Video footage and photos that caught the emotion in my eyes probably led folks to believe that I had been so moved by Sarah's speech, but now you know that I was sharing a moment with my boy.

At the conclusion of Sarah's speech, we each cycled through the crowd gathered about the stage, shaking hands, signing autographs and taking pictures. What a wild feeling it was sharing the spotlight with her. Some have suggested that it was the other way around, but I don't believe that for a second, nor do I remotely want to, for that would not bode well for our country. Me, an unemployed plumber taking center stage with possibly the most exciting VP candidate this country has seen since T.R.? That would be an extra-special kind of ridiculousness.

When we finally were able to exit the arena to the locker area again, I was immediately escorted to the Trainers' Room and waited for my family to join me, while Sarah, Todd and her crew went to conduct some interviews that had been setup elsewhere. Soon as I saw Joey walk in the door, I gave him a big long hug. I then embraced my dad, feeling his pride and realizing that he wasn't supposed to have lived long enough to have seen this moment, where his son reached a small pinnacle usually reserved for giants. I had no misgivings about my purpose and my goals, but I would not have been human had I not, in some measure, taken in the profoundness of these events.

After Palin had finished her interviews, I was able to take my son, my dad and my uncle to meet the Governor from Alaska, a woman who had arguably come closer to the power of the presidency than any woman before her.

After graciously greeting my family, Sarah approached me, looked me in the eye and said, "Joe, America needs us to keep working."

Of course, my thought was, *Yes, you are right about that.* I also thought, Can you tell your people to get their butts in gear then, so I can get to work! Instead, I replied, "I agree with you."

That was it. I have not had a chance to meet or speak with her since. I found her to be genuine, vibrant, energizing and magnetic. She was a great speaker and had a commanding presence. Knowing something about her career as Governor in Alaska, I feel comfortable in saying that among the four politicians in the final contest for the highest office in our country, I would have chosen Palin to be president in a heartbeat. If you want to talk about change and the tenacity to see it through, I dare say she was our ticket to real change for the better.

13

Meeting John McCain

The day after the Palin rally was fairly peaceful and a welcomed change of pace next to what had become the norm. I had been discussing an opportunity to meet up with McCain somewhere along the road, most likely Thursday when he came to Ohio. That was logical, and yet I couldn't get a cemented plan from McCain's people to save my life. Come Thursday this somehow resulted in McCain getting up on stage in Defiance, Ohio calling out for me to join him on stage. Unfortunately, I was not there. Now how could such a blunder happen in a contest for the most powerful office in the world, and in the final days no less?

So what happened? As I mentioned earlier, it was like pulling teeth to get definitive plans from the various Republican camps. At first, it was suggested that I go on tour with Palin. Then somebody thought I should go with McCain, seeing how Palin didn't need much help drawing large crowds. Then I met the Jewish man from Florida, after which I got the distinct feeling they just didn't know if I was a Pandora's Box or not. I can answer that. Yes I am, and proud of it!

Anyhow, there was discussion about me meeting up with McCain at Defiance, Ohio to get up on stage with him like I had with Palin. I was plenty willing, but here's the problem; no one confirmed it and no one had a real plan. At first, they told me to drive out so I could hop on the McCain bus for the rest of the day and possibly the week. There's only one problem; Defiance is almost an hour away from where I live in Holland, and no one had a plan for my car. I wasn't just going to park it somewhere and then hitchhike back to it. Remember what happened the last time I left a car somewhere?

So, how did this result in McCain getting up on stage and calling out for me when I wasn't present and didn't know I was supposed to be? Who the heck knows, but it was probably only a symptom of the larger problem that plagued his entire campaign. Every time he gained some momentum, something careless like this would happen and he would lose ground to Obama.

I was out having breakfast at the restaurant where my mom waitresses, when suddenly my phones started ringing uncontrollably again. It was like clockwork. If something happened out on the campaign trail that involved me or use of my name and profession, my phones would start hopping with reporters and interview requests. Reluctantly, I picked up the third or fourth call—by now I was making progress in learning to ignore them a little better. It was CNN and they wanted to confirm if I had now decided to vote for Obama. *What?* That's how I found out McCain had been expecting me, but I had been *Joe The No Show*. I actually had to ask the reporter what happened, if you can believe that—unreal!

Next thing I knew, every Republican Party member in the State of Ohio with my number was calling my cell phone. They practically begged me to meet McCain at his next rally over in Sandusky, Ohio. I tried to tell them I had another commitment that evening in Philadelphia. I had flight arrangements set to attend a policemen's benefit for families of slain officers at Geno's Steaks in South Philly. It had taken a lot of effort to setup that trip, and I really wanted to be there a heck of a lot more than I wanted to stump for anyone. Let's see, hang out with politicians for the day or eat some genuine Philly Cheese Steaks while helping some real people in need? You make the call.

The long and the short of it is that I had little choice but to agree to meet up with McCain. If I didn't show up somewhere that day with him, can you imagine how that would have played amongst the press? Instead of being hailed as a catalyst for his presidential bid, I would be resoundingly blamed for sinking it. Can you believe that, me the plumber tipping the scales? As ridiculous as that sounds, such had become my new reality. I was nearly fed up with the entire political scene at that point. I really wanted nothing more to do with it. Yet, I sucked it up and decided I had better go and do my best.

It was a scramble to get back to my house, pack an overnight bag and clean up a bit before I met a man who could be the next President of the United States. It was also a long drive to Sandusky, and I really questioned if I could make it on time. Can you imagine how a second, *"Joe where are ya?"* would have played out in the media?

Fortunately, we did arrive in downtown Sandusky about forty-five minutes ahead of McCain's *Straight Talk Express*. As we drove around looking for an appropriate place to dismount, the large crowds gathered behind police barriers and cordons occasionally noticed me in the passenger seat and began cheering. We then came upon a street vendor, selling none other than *Joe The Plumber* buttons, and yes with a picture of *Joe The Plumber* on them. The guys that were driving me called the man over and asked if the *real* Joe The Plumber could get a button or two. The man was beside himself and quickly grabbed a fistful to hand over to me. At first I was thinking, *How does this guy put my face on something and sell it without my permission?* But upon closer examination, the photo on the button was not me. It was some other bald guy that had an uncanny resemblance to Mr. Clean. Come to think of it, do I?

We were greeted by a man from McCain's advance team, whose name I don't remember. He was a nice enough guy, and gave me some relief when he said he would be my guide of sorts throughout my participation on McCain's tour that day (he would later disappear and I never saw him again). He led us into the school and down the hall to the administration offices. Everyone was very nice, but I got a distinct cold sensation as I walked through the doors of and into the principal's office. It had nothing to do with the school or the principal. It just felt like I had time-warped back to my childhood, where I spent a little too much time visiting my school principal's office. Does anyone, besides the principal, ever feel at home in the principal's office?

When McCain's *Straight Talk Express* arrived in Sandusky, I was quickly ushered outside the school into Washington Park, where I was greeted by a huge crowd. It didn't take them long to recognize me, and the notion that my life wasn't going to be normal anymore finally seeped through my thick skull. At least, I realized normalcy would not likely return until after the election. When you can't go anywhere without being recognized by folks desperately wanting your picture, autograph, handshake or a hug, some normally basic routines in life have to be thrown out the window.

Amidst the McCain crowd cheering and calling out my name, I was escorted down from the school steps to a position out on the road where the *Straight Talk Express* was planned to stop and Senator McCain would dismount to finally meet Joe The Plumber. As I waited, and yes, took pictures, shook hands and gave autographs, I began to wonder just what I was going to feel in McCain's presence, a man whom I hoped would become president. As I have stated, I deeply appreciated and honored his service in the military, but I also had a great number of issues with him concerning his proposed policies and record in the senate. However, this is what you have to understand about me. I never expect that I am going to absolutely love everything there is to know about a President of the United States. Had I lived during the terms of T.R., Lincoln or Washington, I would have found cause to gripe here and there.

As another ten minutes or so passed by, a group of Secret Service and campaign coordinators showed up to both secure the scene and control its presentation to the national media. What do I mean by control? Well, it's all about the small details, like *The bus needs to stop here* (remember my *bean bag* with Dianne Sawyer?), and *Joe, you need to stand here, facing this way,* and *You* (the media) *need to be over here to catch the first shot of Senator McCain meeting Joe. No, not there, here or the sun won't catch the senator's face right.* Get the picture? Forget about everything you know from what you read in the paper, see on the television or hear on the radio. With but rare exception, everything put forth to the public has been carefully scripted, choreographed, lighted, sound-mixed and staged right down to the last ounce of makeup used to touch up those unsightly blemishes and awful tendencies for the skin to shine or glare on camera. Aside from the words people speak, and you have to listen closely to what people are really saying anymore, you have no concept of what is real. I had always been pessimistic about it myself, as I imagine many of you have been. Nonetheless, nothing could have prepared me for the reality, which is so much worse that we all realize.

In the midst of being positioned and asking a few questions of the coordinators to find out exactly what I was supposed to do and where I was supposed to go—to which I received blank stares—McCain's *Straight Talk Express* appeared from around the corner. With a couple honks from the big horn the crowd went wild and Van Halen's *Right Now* started blaring on the PA system, which personally I thought was a good choice of theme music.

The first one I recognized coming off the bus was Meagan McCain, soon followed by her mother Cindy and then John. Without hesitation, the senator and his wife came over to me. John reached out, shook my hand and then briefly embraced me. He thanked me for coming out and then introduced me to Cindy.

When I turned back to McCain for some direction as to what was next, he was gone. I barely caught sight of him, surrounded by Secret Service, heading for the cordoned crowd. I didn't know what I was supposed to do. Should I stay put, get on the bus for the next stop or follow him? I looked around for some direction, but no one seemed to be in charge of me, so naturally I took charge of me and followed the senator. I was quickly besieged by the crowd and immediately went into *meet the folks* mode, which was the most gratifying thing I did throughout all my travels during this election. These were the real people, with real challenges in life and having a real need for a real leader that wouldn't lead our country down the path of socialism.

I followed the senator along the base of a gazebo centered in the park, from which he was to speak. I heard intermittent chants of *"Joe, Joe, Joe"* and *"McCain, McCain, McCain!"* This was just another surreal moment among a legion of them in the last two weeks. What office was I running for? McCain ascended to the gazebo stage with Cindy beside him, and I wasn't long behind. He addressed the crowd and quickly introduced me as *"The Straight Talker."* I kinda liked that description. It sure beat a lot of what was being said about me in the press and on the Internet. I was happily standing in the background, feeling a great surge of humility and again, hearing the voice in my head saying, *What are you doing here? You are a plumber for Pete's Sake!*

"Joe, why don't you say a few words to the folks," McCain unexpectedly said and reached out to me with the microphone.

I was about ready to jump under the crawlspace of the gazebo for some familiar company. It was a gracious gesture by the senator, and gutsy. After all, I was out in the media saying all kinds of crazy things like, *"Socialism, Scared for America, the Real American . . ."* I wondered what McCain thought I would say, or maybe hoped I would. Perhaps he was under the impression I had been prepped with some talking points. At any rate, I gathered my courage and tried not to look as nervous as I was feeling inside, then told the crowd something to the effect of, *"Get out and get informed before you vote, and don't take anyone else's opinion for your own."* It wasn't exactly the *Get out and vote for McCain!* slogan the Republican Campaign HQ was probably looking for, but it resonated with the crowd well enough. I was on stage with the man on his campaign tour. Did I have to come right out and state the obvious? I hate patronizing people.

McCain went on to give his speech, but also took a moment to chastise those from Obama's campaign and elsewhere who had come out and attacked me. I really did appreciate that. I don't think anyone realized just how bad it had been. When you are in the public eye, you expect some digging through your private life, and snooping about in your personal records. As a public official sworn to serve the American people, that's what is expected and is necessary to minimize government corruption. However, I was just a plumber and had absolutely no resources whatsoever to fight the invasion that came my way. Do you know how much it costs to get a lawyer these days? Let me put it this way, it takes about 6 months of a plumber's income just to get them out of the starting gate. Considering all the outrage on my behalf from the Republican Party, wouldn't you have expected an army of lawyers to have been leaping at the chance to defend me? Not so. As is usually the case in my life, for whatever reason, I was going to have to fight that battle the hard way.

After his speech, the McCains, along with me in tow, made their way through the midst of the crowd and up the school steps for a photo-op with Joe The Plumber, waving to the crowd. We all then went inside the school, where the McCains were quickly guided into a side room by his staff to conduct a television interview. I remained outside in the hall with Secret Service, just passing the time. I listened in on the interview and kind of chuckled to myself, for I was listening live to what the rest of the country, at least those interested and tuned in, would hear later that evening.

Upon concluding the interview, John and Cindy emerged and came over to me. "You're a great American, Joe," he said. "Thank you for coming out."

"You're a great American for your service," I told him.

"Well, thank you. I'm glad to have met you." I heard goodbye in his tone, which surprised me.

"Aren't I coming with you?" I asked.

McCain looked around for his staffers, genuinely confused himself. "Are you?"

"I'm pretty sure that was the plan," I suggested. "I believe I'm supposed to go on the bus with you for a couple more stops."

Some of his staff quickly snapped their attention from the *Borg-buds* in their ears and confirmed the plan.

"Well, okay. Great!" McCain agreed.

With that, he was ushered through the hall and into the school to drop in on a classroom or two, which I thought was pretty cool. His staff advised me that I should stay put and wait for him to come back through before we would go out and load up into the bus.

I had hardly spent any time at all with Governor Palin, but got a small taste of the hustle and bustle schedule these people have to maintain. It must have been nerve-racking and fairly difficult to keep things straight, whether young or old. I realized that the people you keep in your stead are the ones who either make it or break it for you on the campaign trail. Like so many other things in life, the people you associate with have a tremendous bearing on your success or failure. The people you employ to represent you and look after your best interests have an even greater bearing. In my humble opinion, McCain should have had an entirely different campaign leadership team. But I guess that boat is off and sailed now, isn't it.

As promised, McCain circled back through the hall and we exited the school to get on the bus. I was surprised how fast the crowd had dispersed. I suppose if McCain had been Elvis, or perhaps Obama, then people would have lingered a bit longer in hopes of catching another glimpse of a superstar. Well, the park that had been a madhouse without an inch to spare between bodies was now a ghost town.

We quickly got to the bus and I followed the McCains inside. My first thought was, *Okay, let's see what a Presidential Tour Bus looks like.* I had been on the bus with Rob Portman and the *Regular Joes* that other day and thought it was cool, but nothing more than a cramped office space. So, how did I regard the gilded interior and super-luxury of McCain's *Straight Talk Express?* It was plain, cramped and perhaps less in total scope and appointments than the *Regular Joes* bus had been. I'm not sure about it, but my impression was that the campaigns lease these things, paint their slogans on them, and then hit the road. It's probably not cheap, but I was happy that it wasn't an over-the-top, *MTV Cribs*-like experience.

Once on the bus, I followed the McCains to the back, along with a cohort of press. There was a horseshoe-shaped conference table at the very back, where I crammed in between John and Cindy and ten or so press people. The bus surged forward and McCain went right into politician-mode in answering the various questions thrown his way. There was nothing significant in the way of questions or answers that bears repeating, and again, therein lays the problem. Where are all the tough questions? We can't just put these candidates into office without having tested their mettle, and yet we do time and again. Probably the toughest question that was brought up, related to the mix-up earlier in the day, where McCain's call for me to join him on stage went unanswered. What a joke! What the heck does that have to do with the man's ability to run the country?

We were probably fifteen miles down the highway heading to our next venue when the bus suddenly stopped, smack-dab in the middle of the road. I looked out the window and saw that traffic had been stopped from going in either direction. One of McCain's managers came back and advised the press it was time for them to dismount and return to the lowly press buses following us. Okay, I'm making up the lowly part. I never saw the interior of their buses, which were probably near replicas of the *Straight Talk Express*. This appeared to be the press routine after every campaign stop.

Once the press had gone, I could see McCain relax a bit, as well as the rest of his team. He proceeded to engage me in a little small talk . . . He wanted to know how my business was going, to which I had to respond, *"What business?"* He mentioned how great Palin and I (interesting) had been to the campaign, and how important it was that we (he) win. His mind seemed elsewhere for most of the discussion, probably sorting out all he needed to accomplish in the next few days if he were going to stop the Obama *Hope Train*. Let's see . . . Train versus Bus. Not much of a contest after all, was it.

Throughout the discussion, Cindy was poised, mentally engaged in the moment and evaluating. You can see it in her eyes; nothing gets past her, and I like that quality in a potential First Lady. Inevitably, a president will find frequent occasion to take counsel from his wife. It's nice to know what that counsel may entail, or that is derives from wisdom. Don't misunderstand, I thought McCain was sharp and clearly displayed a youthful energy, but his personality was a little more sporadic to me.

The next couple of stops on the campaign trail were basically carbon copies of the first, except that I was with McCain each step of the way. However, I did pay close attention to the content of his speech. The climax of each stop was when he spoke about PORK and how he wouldn't suffer any to cross his desk as president. In fact, he stated with great enthusiasm that anyone who tried to include pork in a bill that came to his desk for signature would be outed. "You will know their names and I WILL MAKE THEM FAMOUS!" he shouted to a roaring crowd time and again. It was noteworthy to me that this was the most inspiring and arousing theme with every crowd of supporters.

Finally, as the press left the *Straight Talk Express* after yet another campaign stop, I couldn't contain myself any longer. I made my way to the back of the bus and sat with McCain and a colleague of his that stumped for him that day.

"Joe, you're doing great out there," McCain began. "I really appreciate it. It's important for America."

"Thanks John," I replied. "Let me just ask you something that's really bugging me."

"Go ahead," he replied graciously.

"Why did you vote for that *bail-out* package, when most of America was against it?" I didn't say it in a disrespectful manner, but I was hot about it and expressed some personal frustration. Before he could answer, I added, "You say you're against PORK, but that bill was loaded with it!"

McCain kind of shrugged and nodded his head in agreement, but said, "I know, I know, but that's the advice we were given, and a lot of them (other senators) didn't want to vote for it. So they had to be coerced into supporting it, and that's where the pork came in."

STOP! Hold the presses, stop the phones and just think for a second. Did you all hear that? *Coerced?* I don't recall the word *coerced* being cited anywhere in our Constitution as a legal means by which our elected representatives are supposed to conduct the people's business. In fact, if you take a moment to look up *coercion* in the dictionary, I think you will agree that it has a negative and decisively criminal feel to it.

"That's just wrong," I told him indignantly. "Also, there were plenty of well-educated economists who didn't support it."

At that point, McCain was looking away and literally waving me off as if annoyed. I'm sure he was. After all, who was I to be grilling him on his own bus? I suppose I should have simply been grateful to be there. I was, or at least had been, just a plumber. How many plumbers got the VIP presidential campaign treatment during this election?

So America, what say you? Does this behavior of mine strike you as being consistent, or something else? That incident with McCain and other discussions with other less admirable political types on the bus that day left me with a worse feeling in my gut about the future of America than did my meeting with Obama. All I could think was, *this is what has become of our country.* I obviously didn't know McCain before he went to serve our country in Vietnam. I didn't know him when he was released from that rat-hole of a prison after being tortured for years, nor have I known him all throughout his career in the senate. However, I am reasonably certain that the good man who went to defend Freedom for his country came back a changed man from his experience, and yet his moral virtue was likely never challenged so much as it has been during his service in the United States Senate. How can you go out and speak against something with such conviction, only to vote it into law a moment later? Ask any senator, congressman or president in the last fifty years and they will all tell you exactly how it is done on Capitol Hill. Whether Democrat or Republican, they all play the same game to conduct the people's business. After all, Obama also voted for the bailout bill, while campaigning on cutting out government wasteful spending. They call it politics.

After the final stop, another speech, another welcoming crowd cheering me along with John McCain, and another opportunity for Joe The Plumber to show his support for the right man to ascend to the Oval Office, I was free to go, thank God.

I made my flight to Philly and was able to quell all the bad from that day with the pure good of giving to others. I have said it before, nothing in life feels better than giving, especially to those who need it. My thanks to Dom Giordano and Ed Palladino of the Big Talker 1210 WPHT for inviting me to be a part of my most rewarding experience of the entire 2008 Presidential Election. Some of you might think that South Philly would be a dangerous place for someone like me, but it was just the opposite. Everyone I met on the street was gracious and kind and I felt blessed to meet each and every one of them. I also could not have picked a better dinner that night than one of Geno's cheese steaks. Thanks Geno, I was hurting something fierce until I found you that night.

That brief, but unequalled experience doing a fundraising appearance in Philly demonstrated for me exactly what *We The People* can do if we put our minds and hearts to it. We can do better than a thousand Obamas and McCains combined. When the big game is over, nobody really cares what party you belong to or which candidate you supported. All that matters is that we are Americans, and we are all in the Biggest Game of Life in our country together.

14

Secure Our Dream

This past Thanksgiving beheld special meaning for a great many Americans, and one can almost hear the prayers of thanks and praise given to God over dinner tables all across this country. At long last, nearly a century and a half after the Emancipation Proclamation, a black man was elected president of our great nation on November 4, 2008. This was indeed a rare and meaningful election year, and it is nothing less than the clear and undisputable manifestation of our American Dream. Truly in this country, no matter what your background or origin, for you anything is possible.

Am I now a Barack Obama banner carrier? Will I now defend the man whose words caused me to fear for the future of my country? Obama will soon be sworn to protect and defend the liberties of our nation with the full force and power of the presidency. Consequently, he may one day during his term find himself in the same position as President Bush, facing the aftermath of a 9-11 and realizing that his defining moments as president and leader of the free world have just begun. When dire, pivotal events strike our president and *us* as a nation, are we to do nothing less than stand behind the man we put into that office? Were there any among you who did not rise in support of President Bush during the early days after 9-11?

During my first trip to New York for Huckabee's show, I made it a point to visit Ground Zero and pay my respects with a moment of silence for those who fell victim to the minions of evil on that tragic day. I felt the gravity of the place, the despair of so many lives lost and the hopes of the countless heroes who have shined since. I realized that my feelings, though strong and deep within my soul, were but a shadow of what our president must have felt as he stood upon that pile of rubble beside the New York City Fire Chief. When he spoke to us about the pursuit of justice that would become his mission, I believed we had, and still have a national calling to action to defend our country against those who would destroy us. If it had been Gore on that hill speaking to us, I would have felt no less.

Yes, I will take up the colors of my president, be he Obama or any other, for the star-spangled banner of the United States of America he bears is also my own. Yes, I shall defend him, for the office he holds stands for the defense of the people of this country who are my family, my friends and my neighbors. The President is the embodiment and enforcement of our Constitution that protects us all. The presidency is greater than any one man, for it transcends politics and any particular man who, for a time, may ascend to its Oval Office. It is our solemn and noble duty to support our president.

I guarantee you that even now, President-elect Obama is swiftly coming to understand the enormity of the burdens that shall soon be transferred from his predecessor's shoulders onto his own. I can imagine he already feels the weight of it. Mark my words, the youthful and vigorous Obama we have seen so much of on television over the past two years will in no wise seem youthful by the passing of his second year as our president. He may have chosen his path in search of greatness and distinction, but it is not a gilded road. *We The People* will ultimately give Obama four of the toughest and most grueling laborious years of his life, for which he will be paid a pittance of what he could earn elsewhere. That should give pause to any of his detractors, as it does me.

Some of you might be scratching your heads right now, but worry not. I will remain vigilant, just as you should. Though the founding principles and ideals of this country are pure, its politicians are not. We have continued to thrive as a nation by virtue of our Constitution and its affinity with the blessings of Almighty God. The greatness of our system of government is that *We The People* hold the balances of power in our nation. If we do not like the performance of our elected president or any other official we put into office during the term of their service, we can vote them out. We are not doomed to live an entire generation under the tyranny of just one man, such as Cuba has experienced under Fidel Castro. When you consider that many citizens of that country have never known freedom and may never come to know it, you have to feel warm all over about America, regardless of who holds office in any given term.

I believed that McCain would have held the line in government a bit better than Obama will, but only time will tell the story of Obama's presidency. I hope it is either remarkably good for our country or plain and unremarkable. Policies that spirit away our freedoms into the hands of socialism for the sake of fairness would be disastrous. For those of you who graduated from the *University of Liberal USA, Why Do I Live Here, I Hate Myself for Being an American for Supposed Higher Learning,* I understand this is exactly what you seek. Nonetheless, let me welcome you to the class of those who will oppose your aims with every ounce of our being in the months and years to come. You are what is wrong with this country. Your version of change will be for the worse, though you have not the wisdom to see it. I dare say the man whom you believed so fervently would usher in those changes will likely disappoint you, the inconsiderate few whose grand visions of societal equality could only result in autocracy. Worry not, for we the quiet and reserved conservative majority in this country understand the nature of your cognitive dysfunction and we shall endeavor to save you from yourselves. It is, after all, the only Christian thing to do.

So what does it mean to take on a cause to Secure Our Dream? It means that no vote should be wasted or never cast. It means that every voice counts and the more voices that share a particular tune the louder and more harmonious they may be heard. As believers in the American Dream and our American way of life, we have to understand that no single election can ever permanently secure and preserve the principles and ideals upon which this country was built. Our foundation as a nation has been weakened by Socialist sappers for decades, and thus it will take decades to repair and refortify. It doesn't really matter if you are a Liberal or Conservative, a Progressive or a Traditionalist, Democrat or Republican. All you must understand is that our country is indeed a beacon of light in the world today, as it has long been throughout the last two centuries. If you come to realize and accept this truth, then you can take heart and appreciate our unique American Values that have made that beacon shine bright. Furthermore, with every given opportunity, you will clearly see the individuals for whom you must vote to ensure the preservation of our American way of life.

My beef is with no one man or woman in government, it is with government as a whole. Our Constitution says WE THE PEOPLE and not we the government for a reason. Without exception in history, unmitigated power to government breeds evil and destruction to life, to enterprise and to the basic innate human pursuit of prosperity. Let us not sell each other into slavery. Let us not cast our pearls to swine. Let us not put all our trust in the wisdom of Washington D.C. Has that not become an oxymoron? Could that city be more unlike the man for whom it was named?

Our elected officials need to be reminded who put them in office and whom they serve each time they start to do something that threatens our American Dream now or for our children in the future. It matters not whether they are Republicans and Democrats, for they are one and the same anymore. They belong to the same elite country club, shop at the same designer stores, understand the differences in types of caviar, and yet they are all addicted to PORK.

When someone asks an elected official a simple question and hence becomes the subject of countless personal attacks and untoward investigative scrutiny by various media and political operatives, something has gone very wrong in our country. When Free Speech has ceased to stand as an inalienable right, unless it is acceptable to the political correctness police, then something has got to change. When Freedom of Religion somehow excludes One Nation Under God, the essence and ideals of our freedoms are seriously in danger. When the forces of government corruption, corporate greed and media bias squelch out the will of the American People, it's time to fight back!

I, along with family, friends and neighbors all across this great country of ours, have founded an organization dedicated to sustaining the voice of the people, to hold our elected officials accountable, and to restore the founding principles and ideals that have made this country great. We believe in the fighting American spirit, that success is born through hard work and determination, and that limited government is essential to the basic freedoms of average Americans. We have come together to fight for the American Dream, knowing that failure to do so will only result in the enslavement of our children and so many more generations in the future. Our time is now, for an opportunity tomorrow may never come. Will we be that generation our children come to hold responsible for our careless neglect of their birthright for liberty? If staying true to the course our Founding Fathers set forth for this country means that we, today, must set aside every frivolous pursuit or desire that catches our whim, so be it. We dare not fail the memory of those great men and women that came before us and sacrificed so much for our future. Shame on us should we fail to sacrifice all we must to secure the futures of those who will be born on this soil or come to this country seeking the American Dream hereafter.

I call upon you, here and now, to join us at secureourdream.com and let us take up Old Glory together and defend our American

Dream. If enough of us demand *real change,* beyond campaign slogans, then Real Change will come. It has happened before and it can happen again. It takes patience, hard work, and adherence to the principles for which this country was founded under God.

If there is one thing I learned at the beginning of this 2008 election experience that rang true throughout and continues to hold steady today, is that there are more of us than there are of those we must oppose. Our only challenge is that they have been more committed, more focused and more consistent in their mission than we. We, by contrast, have been doing the business of America, and by doing so, have sustained her greatness. Yet, now we must put aside our axes and our shovels, our laptops and cell phones and take to the streets once more. These times in which we now live demand a renewed commitment to service and sacrifice for the American Values, Principles and Ideals to which we hold true. Leaders must arise from among us and come into the light. Some may need to work their deeds in their neighborhood, some in their state and some on Capitol Hill. Who will accept the challenge and come forth? I will, and I hope that you join me.

T.R. used to say, *"Believe you can and you're halfway there."* It's akin to a common refrain from my father, which was, *"Can't never accomplished anything."* Though the road may be long and a hard fight ahead, *We The People* must stop apologizing for being American. By coming together at secureourdream.com, we will embark on a journey where we will shout from the highest rooftops all across this great nation that "We are proud to be Americans, and we will fight to keep our American Dream!"

POSTSCRIPT

Joe The Plumber

If there is one thing I learned throughout this experience, it's that I really enjoyed being a plumber. There is another world out there that many of us hardly know, nor do we much understand. After a small taste of that other dimension in life called politics, I decided I didn't like it, I didn't enjoy it, and I hardly found any redeeming qualities about it. Nonetheless, our engagement in the political process in this country is essential to our present wellbeing and the future we leave for our children. In that respect, I suppose politics is a good metaphor for the hard work we all dislike, yet must often do in order to provide a better life for our loved ones.

The silver lining to this story is that I found purpose, and it called out to me from a place I had known long before *Joe The Plumber* entered your living rooms through your televisions and radios. In hard times, I found strength through my faith in God, love through my family, and moral support through my neighbors in every city or town I have visited during this journey. You all reminded me how great this country is and why it is worth fighting for. I thank all of you for that from the bottom of my heart.

So what's next for *Joe The Plumber?* Well, Joe Wurzelbacher needs to get back to work. Doing some plumbing work for a friend here or there is fulfilling, and you now know how fond I am of manual labor, but it most assuredly does not put food on the table, nor will it keep a roof over my family's heads. However, I have found a new profession, and it is all about working for you. You may have heard, and certainly read within the last chapter of this book, that I have put together an organization that I hope will bring regular folks together to fight for our American Dream. You can visit my website at secureourdream.com to learn all you need to know about it. I hope you will do so today and register to become a part of an exciting movement.

Secureourdream.com is a community of Americans who are concerned about the direction in which our country is leaning, and like you, they want to do something about it. Through this organization I hope to bring enough of us together to successfully keep a watchful eye on government. I would also like to see us come up with a variety of meaningful community-based solutions for those in our country who are stricken with the tough economy, or may be suffering from things much worse. We have a great head start from an outpouring of registered supporters, but more of you are needed to truly make this a meaningful and powerful endeavor.

One of the initiatives that falls at the top of my agenda, and is directly related to the state of the economy, is the Fair Tax. It seems to me that Democrats have a point when they say that the so-called rich in this country are not paying their fair share of our national financial burden. However, Republican pursuits for lower taxes and smaller government also greatly appeal to me. Here's a novel idea; let's establish a tax system that is equally and proportionately applied across economic means, while at the same time reducing the tax burden by shrinking the size of government. Makes sense, doesn't it?

Let me see a show of hands, who likes the IRS? Hello, anyone out there . . . As one of the single largest government agencies in the United States, how many of your feelings will be hurt if we dramati-

cally reduce its size in proportion to the elimination of its adminis-
trative burden—that means cutting IRS jobs? Anyone . . . Lawmak-
ers on Capitol Hill could in any legislative year implement a simpler
and fairer tax code. Why don't they? My guess is that most of the
folks on Capitol Hill are rich, so they really don't want to see a tax
system that requires them to pay more of their fair share of the tax
burden, and that's on both side of the political aisle. I suppose it also
has something to do with power. You see, when government grows,
the last thing people in government want to see is their empire
shrink. It's just human nature. Moreover, who among you wants to
see your colleagues lose their jobs? I don't, but I bet we could all find
some replacement jobs in the private sector for those nicer folks that
work for the IRS. I suppose we can find some jobs for the jerks too.
Being a plumber, many qualifying positions come to mind for those
especially deserving individuals. Regardless, does the Federal
Government have any business being the single largest employer in
the United States? Well, it is . . .

I won't go into length here about what sort of Fair Tax I think
this country needs and how it will restore our economy faster than
anything our politicians can muster. Just go to secureourdream.com
and signup (you can do so for free) so that you can begin to take part
in our community discussion to organize around this initiative and
many more worthy causes. Together, I think we can make a real
difference where so many have failed before. It only takes just a tiny
bit of your time to make a GREAT BIG difference for us all, so
don't wait. Get out to secureourdream.com today and let's get to
work for America!

ACKNOWLEDGEMENTS

I would like to take this opportunity to thank PearlGate Publishing, LLC and my friend and publisher Thomas N. Tabback, along with his beautiful family. When this all began, money was thrown at me left and right for my story, hence my opportunity to "cash in." Thomas instead came to me and said, "Let's do something with meaning." That was all it took for me, because I knew he was sincere. One of the many blessings this experience brought about is my friendship with Thomas and his family.

Throughout this rollercoaster ride on the 2008 Presidential Election, my family and my friends sustained me during dark and challenging times. Thank you all so much for you support, your love, your prayers and your patience. Robert, you have always been there for me. I admire your dedication to your children and I think you are a Great Dad. I am very proud of our relationship and to have you for my brother. Uncle Randy, thank you for giving it to me straight. You don't sugarcoat anything. If I'm doing something stupid, you say, "Joe pull your head out of you butt!" I love you for that, and I needed that voice of reason. You're as real as they come. Uncle Emil, I know you're dead, but I know you're looking down on us. I hope I make you proud. I miss your help with building things, but mostly I miss your cooking. Uncle Phil, aside from our shared interest in country music, what I love about you most is that you can walk into a convenience store and become friends with the clerk five minutes later. I needed an extra helping of that skill during this ordeal, and I really appreciate your advice and the example you set for me.

Doug and Jennifer, thank you both for being my friends and for sticking by me all these years. During this interesting time in my life, both of you helped me stay on the straight and narrow. You both are always looking out for me and I really appreciate it.

My thanks and gratitude to Robert, Beth, Aron and Allen for your continued support in seeing secureourdream.com come to life. Also, thank you Aaron Tippin for your friendship and continued counsel since we first met on Huckabee.

There are many in the media and those I met on the campaign trail, whom I'd like to acknowledge as well. First, let me thank Geno of *Geno's Steaks* in Philly, Dom Giordano and Ed Palladino of WPHT Radio 1210AM "The Big Talker" for approaching me with the opportunity to assist with the charity event for the families of police officers slain in the line of duty. That was one of the most important, if not the most important thing I did during the election.

Let me extend my special thanks and appreciation to Neil Cavuto of Fox News, Katie Couric of CBS and Diane Sawyer of ABC for graciously introducing me to the mainstream media. I have learned something from each of you, and I thank you for the positive experience. I wish all the media could have as much class as you all demonstrate regularly on your programs.

To my friends in Talk Radio, I can't say enough. You all have been the absolute best and truly made me feel supported when times got tough. I'd like to express my personal appreciation to Glenn Beck, Mike Gallagher, Larry Elder, Tammy Bruce, Bill O'Reilly, Lou Dobbs, John Gibson, Bill Cunningham, Greg Knapp, Tom and Mike Tabback at KAZM, and the many more who have either had me on your program or have given me your vocal support. Above all, thank you Laura Ingraham for being my staunchest ally, for your fighting spirit for true conservatism, and for helping me launch my bid for Congress in 2010.

To the folks at Fox News, and particularly to producers like Megan, Jesse, Michelle, Kim, Lindsay and so many others, thank you so much for your help, your patience, and your hospitality during each of my visits to New York. My special thanks to Bill O'Reilly for taking a keen interest in the State of Ohio, and to Megyn Kelly and Lis Wiehl for your time and interest as well. Thank you Hannity and Colmes for showing me how to have fun with politics, which I had not thought was possible. Let me give a warm hello and thanks out to the whole crew at Fox & Friends. You all have been great and I appreciate your support. Lastly, I'd like to extend a special thanks to Governor Huckabee for bringing me onto your program again and introducing me to Tito The Builder!

Tito, I was glad to meet you and I hope we can do much with secureourdream.com together in the future. Your support for me means more than you can know, and I want you to know that I support YOU. God bless you and your family.

Thanks to Deborah Norville, Carl Bevelhymer and the folks at Inside Edition. Thanks to Christopher Liss and team over at EXTRA. Thanks to Dave Patton and the folks at Newsmax, and every other member of the media out there who treated me fairly and with kindness in America and around the world. There are plenty of you *good guys* out there in newspapers, on television and on the Internet. I really do appreciate your commitment to honest and accurate reporting.

On the campaign trail, let me thank the Secret Service first and foremost for keeping us all safe! I'd also like to thank the good people of John McCain's, Sarah Palin's, Steve Chabot's and Jean Schmidt's campaign teams. You guys were the sunlight amidst an otherwise gray and overcast political atmosphere. Also, thank you to the *Regular Joes* in Ohio; Mary the Flag Lady, Mike the Painter, Cathy the Pool Supply Lady, Lucy the Florist, Linda the Fitness Trainer, The Cupcake Couple and everyone who participated on that tour that day. You guys are an inspiration to me, as I imagine you are to American Dreamers everywhere.

My special thanks to Sarah Palin for your graciousness and for instilling some faith in me that true conservatism remains alive and well in this country.

Before I forget, thank you President-elect Barack Obama and Senator John McCain, for making my 2008 Election Year experience profound beyond my wildest imagination. Thanks to you both, I have discovered new purpose in my life, and I can't go to the bathroom anywhere in America without being asked for an autograph. You guys are the greatest!

Above all, thank you to the American People who have supported me since Joe The Plumber became a media spectacle. First and foremost, I am an American, just like you. I could not have endured all that I did without your kind words, your letters of encouragement, and all the ways in which you have expressed your support. Thank you for buying this book and please go to secureourdream.com to join our fight to protect and defend our American Dream!

PEARLGATE

We Are Your Publisher

At PearlGate, we believe that all gifts of talent are endowed by God, and that literature, in particular, possesses a unique ability to ignite the spirit of our fellow brothers and sisters. We therefore seek to publish written works that exhibit a spark that will ignite our human spirit. We sincerely hope you have found this quality within these pages.

As a small publisher, we are greatly dependent upon your referrals. If you enjoyed this book, please spread the word about all of PearlGate's titles (www.pearlgatepublishing.com) to your family, your friends, colleagues, social and religious groups, and anyone you meet who may give you their ear. If you don't find our titles at your local bookstore, ask the store manager to carry them. Amidst today's rigid publishing standards, were it not for publishers like PearlGate, this poem by Phillis Wheatley (1753-1784) might never have found its way onto bookshelves . . .

Twas mercy brought me from my Pagan land,
Taught my benighted soul to understand
That there's a God, that there's a Saviour too:
Once I redemption neither sought nor knew,
Some view our sable race with scornful eye,
"Their colour is a diabolic die."
Remember, Christians, Negroes, black as Cain,
May be refin'd, and join th' angelic train.

ABOUT THE CO-AUTHOR

Thomas N. Tabback was born in North Carolina while his father was stationed with the Army at Fort Bragg. Later, his parents moved to Arizona where he grew up and discovered his passion for writing at an early age. When he was twelve, he wrote his first short story and never put down the pen.

Thomas began his collaboration with Samuel J. Wurzelbacher shortly after the third and final 2008 Presidential Debate. From the time he and *Joe The Plumber* teamed up, Thomas witnessed firsthand the perpetual media blitz, the revelation of the Ohio State illegal violation of Joe's privacy, the initiation of the *Joe The Plumber Bus Tour*, Joe's meeting with Sarah Palin, and his subsequent meeting with John McCain on the *Straight Talk Express*. With his penetrating writing style and eyewitness perspective into the story of *Joe The Plumber*, Thomas has painted a vivid and captivating portrayal of a quintessential Middle-Class American who was unexpectedly swept into perhaps the most pivotal presidential election of our lifetime.

Thomas and his wife of thirteen years met and married while they worked a summer job at Universal Studios Hollywood. They now live in Austin, TX with their four children, where he writes amidst the beauty of the Hill Country.

Don't miss Thomas N. Tabback's debut novel . . .

Available now at a bookstore near you or go to
www.thingsforgottenbook.com

PearlGate Publishing